Street by Street

SALISBURY

AMESBURY, WILTON

Alderbury, Bishopstone, Bulford, Coombe Bissett, Downton, Durrington, Great Durnford, Great Wishford, Larkhill, Porton, Redlynch, Shrewton, Stapleford, Stonehenge, Winterbourne Gunner

C000024072

1st edition January 2003

© Automobile Association Developments Limited 2003

Ordnance Survey® This product includes map data licensed from Ordnance Survey® with the permission of the Controller of Her Majesty's Stationery Office. © Crown copyright 2003. All rights reserved. Licence No: 399221.

Published by AA Publishing (a trading name of Automobile Association Developments Limited, whose registered office is Millstream, Maidenhead Road, Windsor, Berkshire SL4 5GD. Registered number 1878835).

The Post Office is a registered trademark of Post Office Ltd. in the UK and other countries.

Schools address data provided by Education Direct.

One-way street data provided by:

Tele Atlas © Tele Atlas N.V.

Mapping produced by the Cartographic Department of The Automobile Association. A01549

A CIP Catalogue record for this book is available from the British Library.

Printed by GRAFIASA S.A., Porto, Portugal

The contents of this atlas are believed to be correct at the time of the latest revision. However, the publishers cannot be held responsible for loss occasioned to any person acting or refraining from action as a result of any material in this atlas, nor for any errors, omissions or changes in such material. This does not affect your statutory rights. The publishers would welcome information to correct any errors or omissions and to keep this atlas up to date. Please write to Publishing, The Automobile Association, Fanum House (FH17), Basing View, Basingstoke, Hampshire, RG21 4EA.

Ref: ML141

Key to map pages	ii-iii
Key to map symbols	iv-1
Enlarged scale pages	2-3
Street by Street	4-41
Index – towns & villages	42
Index – streets	43-46
Index – featured places	46-47

ii

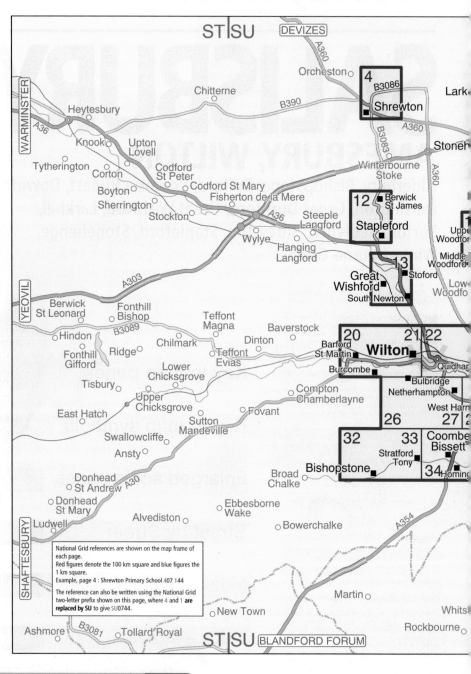

ST|SU   DEVIZES

WARMINSTER

A360

Orcheston

Chitterne

4   B3086

Heytesbury

B390

Shrewton

Lark

A36

B3083

A360

Knook

Upton Lovell

Winterbourne Stoke

Stoneh

Tytherington

Corton

Codford St Peter

Boyton

Codford St Mary

Fisherton de la Mere

12   Berwick St James

Sherrington

A36

Steeple Langford

Stapleford

Upp Woodfo

Stockton

Wylye

Hanging Langford

Middle Woodford

13

A303

Great Wishford

Stoford

Low Woodfo

YEOVIL

South Newton

Berwick St Leonard

Fonthill Bishop

Teffont Magna

Baverstock

B3089

Hindon

Chilmark

Dinton

Barford St Martin

20

21 22

Wilton

Fonthill Gifford

Ridge

Teffont Evias

Burcombe

Quidhar

Tisbury

Lower Chicksgrove

Compton Chamberlayne

Bulbridge

Netherhampton

East Hatch

Upper Chicksgrove

Fovant

West Harn

Sutton Mandeville

26

27

Swallowcliffe

32

33

Coombe Bissett

Ansty

Stratford Tony

A30

Bishopstone

34 Homing

Donhead St Andrew

Broad Chalke

Donhead St Mary

Ebbesborne Wake

A354

SHAFTESBURY

Ludwell

Alvediston

Bowerchalke

National Grid references are shown on the map frame of each page.
Red figures denote the 100 km square and blue figures the 1 km square.
Example, page 4 : Shrewton Primary School 407 144

The reference can also be written using the National Grid two-letter prefix shown on this page, where 4 and 1 **are replaced by SU** to give SU0744.

Martin

B3081

Ashmore

Tollard Royal

New Town

Whits

Rockbourne

ST|SU   BLANDFORD FORUM

Enlarged scale pages   1:10,000   6.3 inches to 1 mile

| 0 | 1/4 | miles | 1/2 |
| 0 | 1/4 | 1/2 | kilometres | 3/4 | 1 |

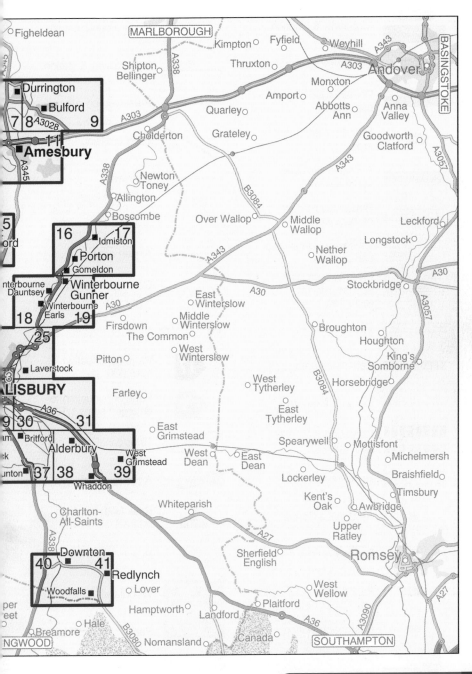

Symbol	Description	Symbol	Description
Junction 9	Motorway & junction	⊖	Underground station
Services	Motorway service area	⊖	Light railway & station
	Primary road single/dual carriageway	++++++++++	Preserved private railway
Services	Primary road service area	LC	Level crossing
	A road single/dual carriageway	•—•—•—•—•	Tramway
	B road single/dual carriageway	- - - - - - - - -	Ferry route
	Other road single/dual carriageway	....	Airport runway
	Minor/private road, access may be restricted	- · - · - · -	County, administrative boundary
← ←	One-way street	ꝟꝟꝟꝟꝟꝟ	Mounds
	Pedestrian area	17	Page continuation 1:15,000
============	Track or footpath	3	Page continuation to enlarged scale 1:10,000
■■■■■■■ ■■■■■■■	Road under construction		River/canal, lake, pier
⊦= = = =⊣	Road tunnel		Aqueduct, lock, weir
AA	AA Service Centre	465 ▲ Winter Hill	Peak (with height in metres)
P	Parking		Beach
P+🚌	Park & Ride		Woodland
🚌	Bus/coach station		Park
	Railway & main railway station		Cemetery
	Railway & minor railway station		Built-up area

	Featured building		Abbey, cathedral or priory
	City wall		Castle
A&E	Hospital with 24-hour A&E department		Historic house or building
PO	Post Office	Wakehurst Place NT	National Trust property
	Public library	M	Museum or art gallery
i	Tourist Information Centre		Roman antiquity
	Petrol station Major suppliers only		Ancient site, battlefield or monument
†	Church/chapel		Industrial interest
	Public toilets		Garden
	Toilet with disabled facilities		Arboretum
PH	Public house AA recommended		Farm or animal centre
	Restaurant AA inspected		Zoological or wildlife collection
	Theatre or performing arts centre		Bird collection
	Cinema		Nature reserve
	Golf course	V	Visitor or heritage centre
▲	Camping AA inspected		Country park
	Caravan Site AA inspected		Cave
	Camping & caravan site AA inspected		Windmill
	Theme park		Distillery, brewery or vineyard

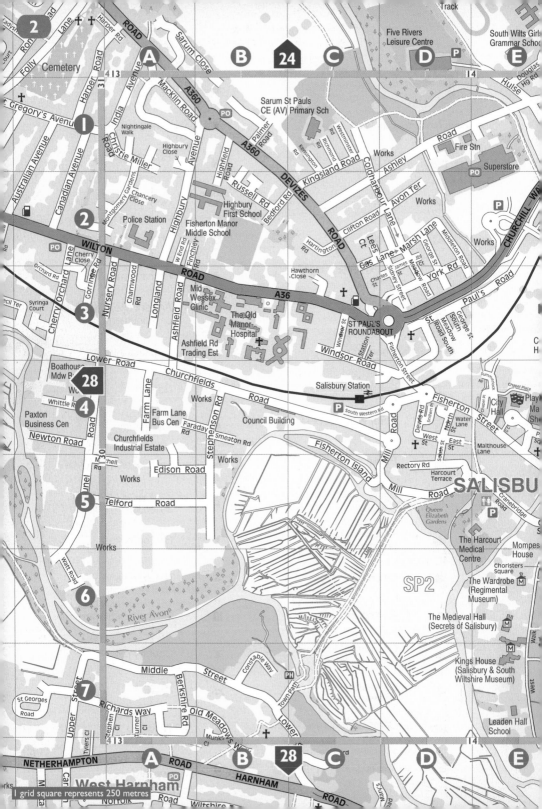

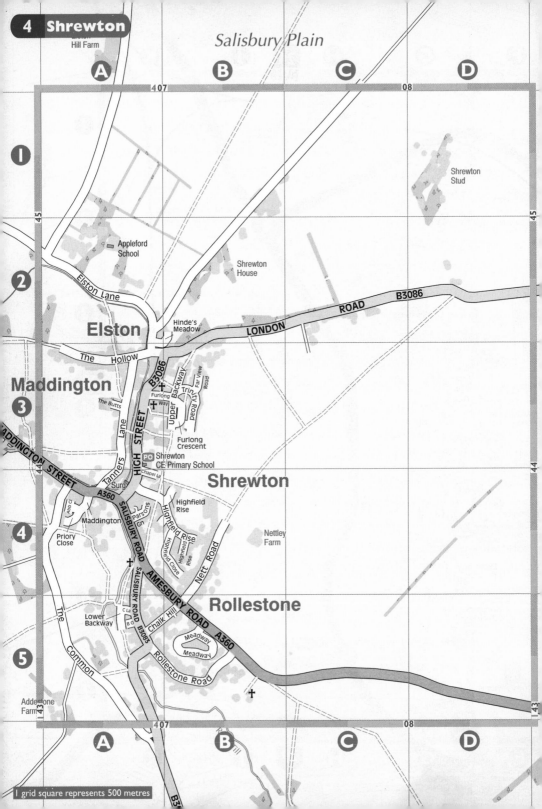

Salisbury Plain

A B C D

4 07 08

1

Elston
Hill Farm

Shrewton
Stud

45 45

Appleford
School

Shrewton
House

2

Elston Lane

ROAD B3086

LONDON

Elston

Hinde's
Meadow

The Hollow

Maddington

3

B3086

The Butts

HIGH STREET

Upper Backway

Far View Road

Trinity Road

Furlong Way

Furlong
Crescent

Tanners Lane

Shrewton

PO Shrewton
CE Primary School

ADDINGTON STREET

44 44

Chapel La

Surg

A360

Abb Cl

Maddington

Parsons Gn

Highfield
Rise

SALISBURY ROAD

Highfield Rise

Highfield Close

Highfield Rise

Nett Road

Nettley
Farm

4

Priory
Close

The Common

AMESBURY ROAD A360

C La

B3083

Lower
Backway

Chalk Hill

Rollestone

Meadway

Meadway

Rollestone Road

5

Addestone
Farm

43 43

A B C D

4 07 08

412   13   14

A   **B**   **6** **C**   **D**

The Avenue

P

A344

Stonehenge

A303

I

2

West Amesbury

3

10

4

Normanton

5

Springbottom Farm

412   13   14

A   **B**   **C**   **D**

Wilsford   Wilsford Farm

I grid square represents 500 metres

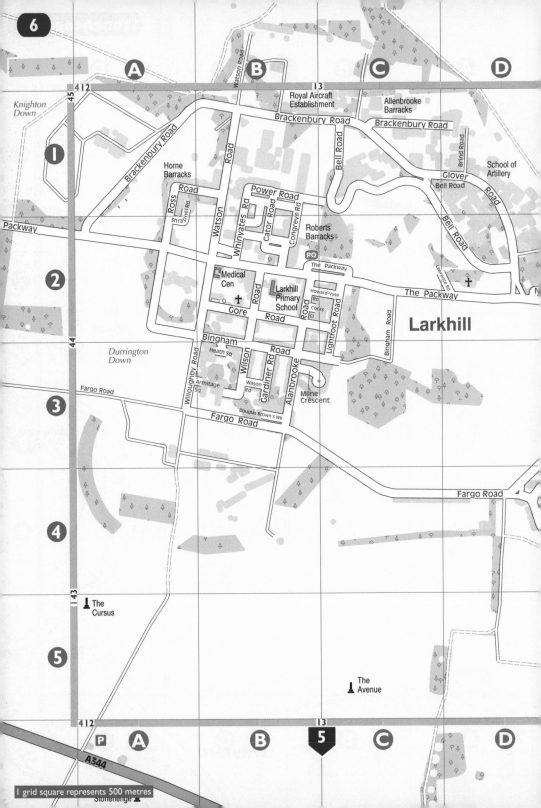

6

A   B   C   D

45   412   13

Knighton Down

Royal Aircraft
Establishment

Allenbrooke
Barracks

Brackenbury Road   Brackenbury Road

1

Horne
Barracks

Brackenbury Road

School of
Artillery

Glover

Bell Road

Brind Road

Road

Ross Road

Power Road

Watson Road

Whinyates Rd

Cator Road

Congreve Rd

Shrapnel Rd

Roberts
Barracks

Bell Road

Low Price Rd

Packway

PO

The Packway

2

44

Medical
Cen

Larkhill
Primary
School

Howard-Vyse
Rd
Cocks
Cl

The Packway

Larkhill

Road

Gore Road

Road

Lightfoot Road

Bingham Road

*Durrington
Down*

Bingham

Heath Sq

Wilson Road

Cardiner Rd

Alanbrooke

Milne
Crescent

Willoughby Road

Armitage Sq

Wason Rd

Douglas Brown's Wk

Fargo Road

3

Fargo Road

Fargo Road

4

143

⚑ The
Cursus

5

⚑ The
Avenue

412   13

P   A   B   **5**   C   D

A344

1 grid square represents 500 metres

Stonehenge ⚑

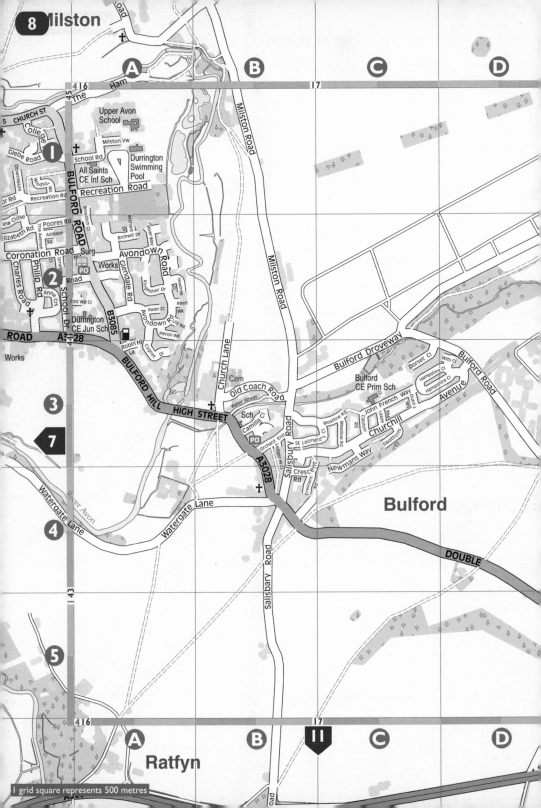

A B C D

The Ham

416
45

CHURCH ST
5
Ollege
Glebe Road
Downleaze
Wmson Ms
or Rd
Recreation Rd

I

BULFORD ROAD

Upper Avon School

School Rd
All Saints CE Inf Sch

Milston Vw

Durrington Swimming Pool

Recreation Road

Milston Road

Bowdich Cl
Brchwd Cl
Brchwd Dr
River Way
Yewtree Cl

New Close
Elizabeth Rd
The Avenue
Addison Sq
Poores Rd
Coronation Road
Philip Rd
Anne Crs
Gramm Cl
Charles Road

Surg
Works
PO

Avondown Road
Glendale Rd
Kingfisher Dr
Swan Cl
Reed Wk
Lily Wk
Cygnet Dr
Heron Wk
Robin Hl La

2

School Dr
B3085
Durrington CE Jun Sch

ROAD A3 28

Milston Road

Works

BULFORD HILL

HIGH STREET

3

7

Church Lane
Cem
Old Coach Road
Water Street
Sch
St Camilla Cl
PO
Orchard End
St Leonard's

Bulford CE Prim Sch
John French Way
Clayton Rd
Cayton Rd
The Leaze
Swatton's
Churchill

Bulford Droveway

Dorset Cl
Wilts Cl
Hampshire Cl
Hampshire Cl

Bulford Road
Avenue

Meadow Rd
Meadow Rd

Newmans Way

Salisbury Road
Crescent
Crescent Rd

A3028

River Avon

Watergate Lane

4

Watergate Lane

Bulford

Salisbury Road

DOUBLE

143

5

416

A B **II** C D

Ratfyn

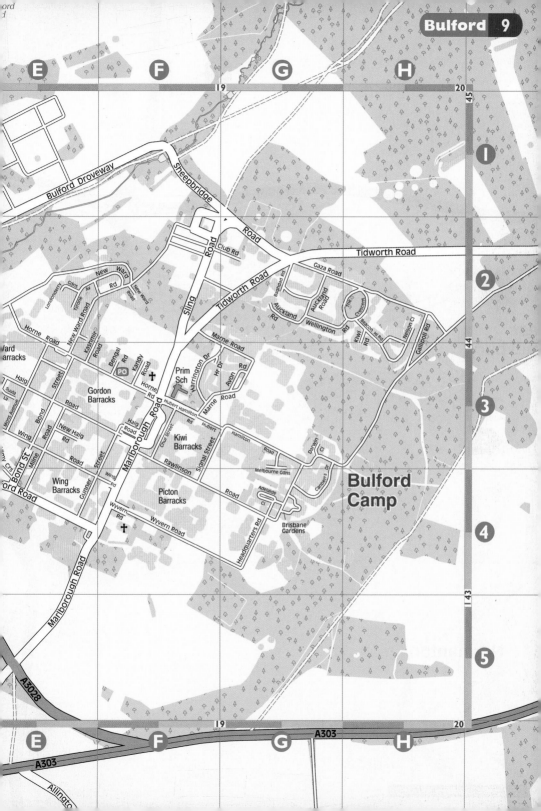

E F G H I

19 20 45

Bulford Droveway

Sheepbridge Road

Club Rd

Tidworth Road

Caza Road

New Ward Rd

Londonderry Gdns

Tyrone Av

New Ward Road

Sling Road

Tidworth Road

Baghdad Rd

Auckland Rd

Auckland Road

Wellington Rd

Kiwi Crescent

Beacon Hi Rd

Nelson Cl

Gallipoli Rd

Horne Road

Kashmir Road

New Ward Road

Bengal Rd

Kandy Road

Horne Rd

Marne Road

PO

Prim Sch

Harrington Dr

Hi Dr

Avon Rd

Marne Road

Ward Barracks

Haig Street

Suvla La

Moors Avenue

Gordon Barracks

Bond Road

Road

New Haig Rd

Marlborough Road

Hubert Hamilton

Chur Street

Hubert

Hamilton Road

Darwin Cl

Bulford Camp

Bond St

Milne Road

Wing Road

Street

Gunner Road

Haig Road

Wing Rd

Kiwi Barracks

Signal Street

Rawlinson Road

Melbourne Gdns

Canberra Dr

Wing Barracks

Crs

ford Road

Picton Barracks

Wyvern Rd

Wyvern Road

Headquarters Rd

Adelaide Cl

Brisbane Gardens

Marlborough Road

A3028

A303

A303

Allingto

19 20

44

2

3

143

4

5

E F G H

E   F   8   G   H

17

Ratfyn

A303

Amesbury Road

A3028

I

42

Amesbury Industrial Estate

London Road

Porton Road

Boscombe Down Business Park

The Pennings

Earl's Farm Down

2

Works

James Road

Queensberry Road

Mills Way

Holders

Antrobus Road

Amesbury

Carpenter Dr

Amesbury Road

3

Orchard Way

Butterfield Drive

Pointers Way

Chesterfield Cl

Raleigh Crescent

Butterfield Drive

Fosters Bshs

Hamilton Cl

Coniston Cl

Tanners Field

Raleigh

Jaggard VW

Pilots VW

Lyndhurst Road

Ringwood Avenue

Beaulieu Road

Boscombe Rd

Beaumont Way

Milton Road

Road

41

Evergreen Way

Flit Crt

Imber Avenue

Cadnam Crs

North Road

Underwood Drive

Harvard WW

Mckle Rd

Ashley Wk

Earls Cl

4

Chambers Avenue

Romsey Rd

Winchester Close

Allington Way

Wilcot Close

Main Road

Orford Road

Martlesham Road

Bawdsey Rd

Stockport Road

5

E   F   G   H

17   18

Boscombe Down Airfield

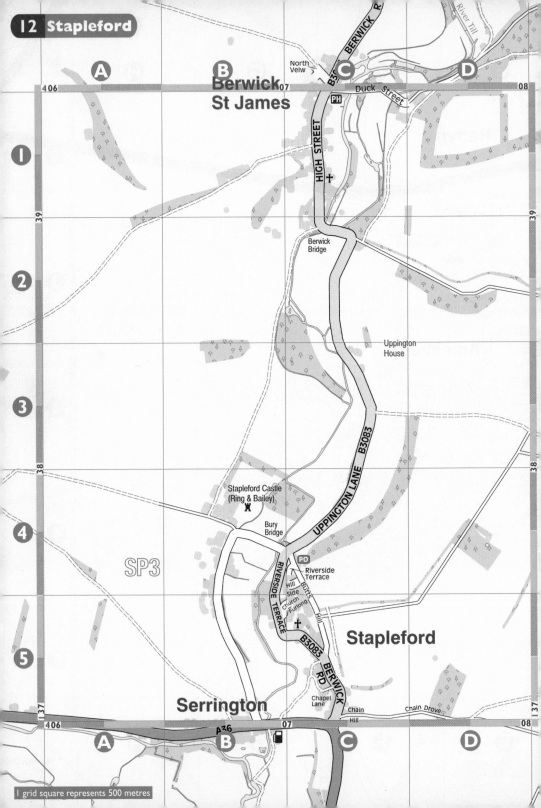

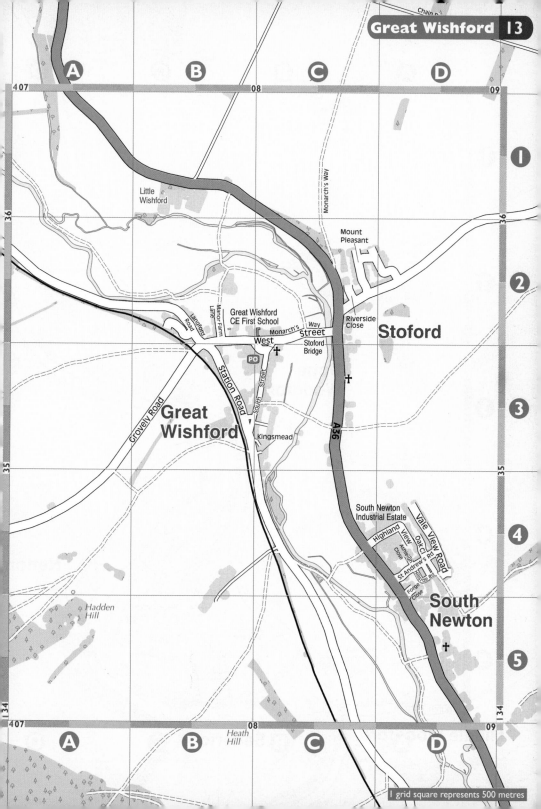

A B C D

407 08 09

I

36 36

2

Stoford

3

Little Wishford

Monarch's Way

Mount Pleasant

Manor Farm Lane

Landford Road

Great Wishford CE First School

Monarch's Way

West Street

Stoford Bridge

Riverside Close

PO

South Street

Great Wishford

Grovely Road

Station Road

Kingsmead

A36

35 35

4

South Newton Industrial Estate

Highland View

Ashleigh Close

Oak Cl

St Andrew's Rd

Vale View Road

Forge Close

South Newton

Hadden Hill

5

A B C D

407 08 09

134 134

A **B** **C** **D**

Heath Hill

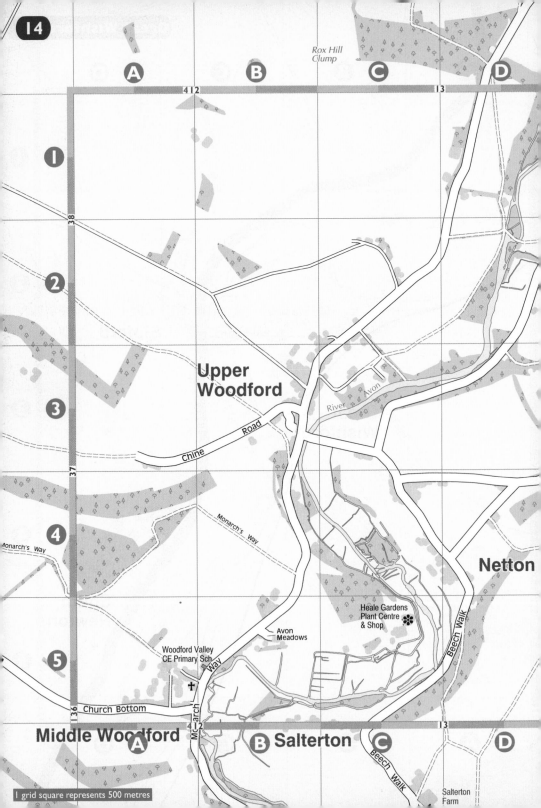

14

A   **B**   **C**   **D**

Rox Hill
Clump

412   13

1

38

2

**Upper
Woodford**

River Avon

3

Chine   Road

4

Monarch's   Way

37

Monarch's Way

Netton

5

Woodford Valley
CE Primary Sch

Avon
Meadows

Heale Gardens
Plant Centre
& Shop

Beech Walk

136   Church Bottom

Monarch Way

412   13

Middle Woodford   **A**   **B** **Salterton**   **C**   **D**

Beech Walk

Salterton
Farm

1 grid square represents 500 metres

Manor House

E 14 F G 15 H

+

Ogbury

I

Great Durnford

38

2

Jubilee Hill

Dow

A345

3

37

Golf Course

4

High Post

Works

High Post Golf Club

5

Works

136

HILL

E 14 F G H
Salterton Down

FOURMILE

15

A338

E   F   G   H

20   21   38

Rivermead

Church

Markan
Road

Church
Road

Church
Rd

LC

Northway

Southway

Blackbarn Road

136

20   21

East   E   F   Feldon Road   G   Porton   H
Down

I

2

37

3

4

5

18

A   416   B   C   17   D

1

Hurdcott Farm

35

Winterbourne Dauntsey

Monarch's Way

Morgan's Lane

2

narch's Way

Portway

Tanners Lane

Winterbourne Earls

Monarch's Way

Hurdcott-Lane

3

34

Monarch's Way

Hurdcott

Northside

†

Green Lane

Lysander

Spitfire

Rd

Rd

The Close

Black Horse Lane

4

Westside

Southside

Old Sarum Business Park

ess Park

5

arum rome

Manor Farm Road

on Dr

Green Lane

Ford

Greenlane Close

33

Merrifield Rd

The Steadings

Ashlands

416

A   B   **25**   C   17   D

338

1 grid square represents 500 metres

Down Barn Cl
Windmill Lane
Mill Close
Gomeldon Primary Sch

E **F** 16 **G** **H**

East Gomeldon Road

Broadfield Rd
Br Cl 19

East Gome

Gomeldon Road

Ladysmith

Hillside Dr

Broadfield Farm

I

35

Horse Barrow

Salt Lane

Elliott's Green

Winterbourne Gunner

Trenchard Av

Thorneydown Road

Allenby Rd

Thorneydown Road

Figsbury Ridge

Thorneydown Road

2

A338

Paddock Cl

Kingsbourne Cl

Monarch's Way

Barracks

Thorneydown Road

Thorneydown

3

34

Road

bury Rd

Figsbury Ring

4

Monarch's Way

se Lane

Bracknell-Croft

A30

Monarch

5

Stock Bottom

133

Shortengrove

A   B   C   D

33   4 06   07

1

2

32

3

Dairy Rd

St Martin's Close

B3089 WEST STREET

Mount Lane

short Lane

Cem

Groveley Road

PH

Barford St Martin
CE First School

Duck Lane

WILTON ROAD

A30

The Cleeves

Barford
St Martin

4

SHAFTESBURY ROAD A30

31

Burcombe

5

Manor House

406   07

A   B   C   D

I grid square represents 500 metres

Chilhampton

E   F   G   H

08   09

Heath Wood

Grovely Hill

33

I

WARMINSTER

Elizabeth Road

Wishford Road

Olivier Rd

Phillip Road

Water

Ditchampton

2

32

Kingsway Business

Wilton CE Middle School

The Hollows

3

Ditchampton

22

St John's Court

Wiley Terrace

Works

Castle Rd

Castle Lane

Victoria Road

Vector Cl

SHAFTESBURY ROAD A30

WEST STREE

NORTH ST

Russe

PO

Ugford

Shortlands

Cemetery

Saddlers Mead

Hlth Cen

SILVER

KINGSB

4

Kingsbury

Wilton

River Nadder

Surgery

131

5

The Crescent

Burcombe

Wilton CE First Sch

Lane

Rawlence Rd

Nddr Ter

Priory Close

Seagrim Rd

Oak Ash Green

Randall's Croft Rd

St Andrew's Close

SA Cl

Randall's Croft Road

St M Cl

St Peter's Close

St Mry's Cl

Swayne Close

Chantry Rd

St Edith

St Andrew's Close

08   09

E   F   G   H

26

ulbridge

St Nicholas Close

Bulbridge

Wessex Rd

Washern Cl

Grovely VW

Hare Cl

South

Home

22

Chilhampton

A 410 **B** **C** **D**

The Avenue

Fug
R

1

33

WARMINSTER

2

32

Kingsway

The Avenue

Ind
Est

Kingsway
Trading
Estate

Kingsway
Business Cen

Works

ROAD

QUEENSTREET A36

Kingsway

Marchment
Close

Thornton
Crescent

Ditchampton

3

**Fugglestone
St Peter**

Fair View Rd

21

Primrose Hill

Kings Gate

Fugglestone

Maple Crsnt

ROAD A30

Wiley
Terrace

KING STREET

Works

Castle
Castle
Lane

Riverside

The Wilton
Shop Village

Church Hill

Whit
Work

Court

Crow La

WEST STREET A30

PO

North Street

Russell St

Council
Building

SALISBURY ROAD A36

4

Hlth Cen

SILVER

Police
Stn

MINSTER STREET

A30

Edgam
Place

Lower Road

Foot's Hill

Wilton

31

SO
KINGSBURY
kingsbury

Nadder
Lane

Hampton
Court

Eveque
Court

Lock's
Lane

ddlers Mead

Oak Ash
Green

Surgery

Wilton
House

Quidhampton

Street

5

HAMPTON ROAD

Wilton
Park

410

A **B** **27** **C** P2 **D**

B3094

I grid square represents 500 metres

Hilltop Business Park

Hill Farm

E

one

F

New Bo

Avon Bridge

Stratford Bridge

G

The Manor House

H

Phillips Lane

33

12

13

I

Old Saru

DEVIZES ROAD

Sheen Close

Angler Rd

 Avshire Cl

Winford Rd

Rmit Dr

Stratford-sub-Castle Primary School

Works

Old Saru

Grace

2

Stratford-sub-Castle

Ramleaze Drive

Shropshire Drive

Cooks

Rambridge crs

Marvland

Olliver Cl

A360

Cedar Cl

Folly VW

The Valley

St Lawrence

Mill Lane

Miller Close

Stratford Road

32

Westwood Road

Pinewoods Close

Pinewood Way

Winding

Barnards Hill Drive

Primrose Rd

St Michael's Rd

Cheshire Cl

DEVIZES

Eagle Field

Castle Keep

Stratford Road

3

awespeare Rd

Shelley Dr

Hathawy

Verone

Capulet

24

Woodlands First School

Hazel Rd

Rowan Cl

Woodside

Glyndbrn Cl

Heath Road

Queen Mary Road

Herbert Road

Rawlence Rd

erton Heath quins FC

Stanley Little Rd

Surg

PO

Penruddock Close

Gainsborough Close

Trmmnt

Crstmn dr Alxndr

Alexandra Road

Wellington Way

Roberts Road

Crown Cl

ROAD

Avon Middle School

River Avon

4

Five Leis Cen

ON ROAD

Western Way

Pullman

Drive

Road

Festival Avenue

Pembroke

Pembroke Park First School

Queen Road

Empire Road

Centurion

St Michael's Rd

Bowes Lyon Court

Ladysmith

Folly Lane

Harper Rd

Cem

Sarum Close

2

PO

Sarum Pauls CE (AV) Primary School

31

Palmer

Kensing Rd

Westmorl

RdRd

Wor

Bemerton

NW Zealand Av

Roman

Crntn Road

Australian Av

St Gregory's Av

Canadian Av

Christie Miller Rd

India Av

Macklin Road

Highbury

Highbury Avenue

Chancery

Highfield

Russell Rd

Highbury First Sch

DEVIZES ROAD

Ashley Rd

Colchbrou

Cliftn Rd

5

Salisbury & S Wilts Sports Club

Chrc La

St Andrew's Road

Brick La

Pmb Rd

Works

Lower Road

A36

PO

Gramshaw Road

PO

Ch

Gorrin

Cherry Orchard Lane

Fisherton Manor Middle Sch

Police Stn

Hartington Road

Bedford Road

A360

land Rd

Gas La

Charle

Hawthorn Close

12

Bemerton St Johns CE First Sch

E

F

28

G

Boathouse Meadow Bus Pk

13

WILTON ROAD

Charnwood Rd

Longland Rd

Ashfield Rd

H

Trad Est

The Old Manor Hospital

Salisbury Station

Windsor Road

Church

ST-PAUL ROUND

Works

Ford

Old Malthouse Lane

The Steadings

Greenlane Close

A338

A30

Pearce

Way

Kimpton

Monxton Close

Lindford Road

Thomas

St Lukes Close

Way

Sfan Dr

Way

LONDON ROAD A338

St Thomas's Bridge

Hallum Close

Jewel

Hoadly Gr

LONDON ROAD A338

Church Road

Bishops Mead

Bishopdown

Chestnut Close

Works

St Josephs Catholic School

Elm Close

Church Road

St Edmunds CE Girls School & Sports College

Wyvern College

PO

St Andrews CE Primary School

The Green

Riverside Road

Woodland Way

Dalewood Rise

Paddock Wy

Silverwood Drive

Westfield Cl

Boundary Road

Riverside Road

Duck Lane

Hill Road

Park Road

Laverstock Pk

The Avenue

Laverstock

Burroughs Hill

Napier Crescent

Linden Close

Mayfair Road

Queen Manor Farm

Queen Manor Road

The Crescent

Burcombe

Wilton
CE First Sch

Lane

Nddr
Ter

Oak Ash
Green

Rawlence
Rd

Randall's

St Andrew's
Close

St Andrew's
Croft

Priory
Close

Seagrim Rd

A **B** **21** **C** **D**

St Andrew's
Close

Randall's
Road

09 Road

Bulbridge

St M Cl

SA Cl

St M Ry's

Swayne
Road

Chantry Rd

St Edith's Cl

Bulbridge

St Nicholas
Close

Wessex Rd

South Street

Bulbridge

Crovley
Vw

Washern
Cl

STE W

Home

1

30

Upper Folly

Lwr

Oly

2

Hunt's
Down

Warren
Down

3

29

Hare
Warren

4

Old

Shaftesbury

Neale's Barrow

Drove

A **B** **33** **C** **D**

Portfield Road

5

128

Windwhistle

408 09

Portfi

E   F   **22**   G   H

Wilton
Park

SP2

I

A3094   NETHERHAMPTON

A3094   NETHERHAMPTON

Netherhampton

2

Kennels

Netherhampton
Business Centre

NETHERHAMPTON ROAD

Salisbury &
South Wilts
Golf Club

3

Sa
Li
M

Golf Course

28

30

29

4

Coombe
Touring Park

Warren

5

Salisbury
Racecourse

128

Drove Lane

E   F   **34**   G   H

E

Park
Pale

Queen Manor Road

F

Clarendon Way

G

Clarendon Way

H

18

19

Clarendon
Palace

Beechy
Dean
Copse

I

Clarendon Way

30

Manor Road

King
Manor
Hill

Long
Copse

2

Canon Copse

3

29

Clarendon Park

4

Clarendon
House

Shute End

5

Clarendon Road

28

18

19

E

F

38

G

A36

H

Hole
Farm

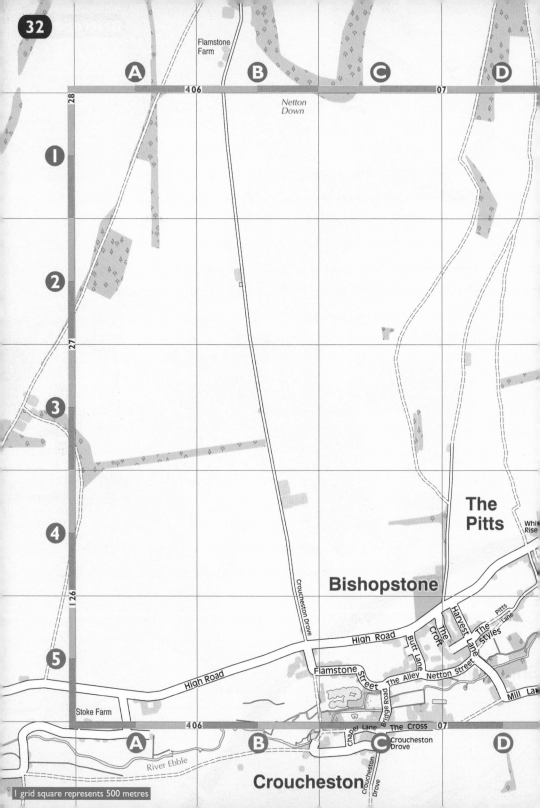

Flamstone Farm

Netton Down

The Pitts

Whit Rise

Bishopstone

Harvest Lane

The Croft

The Styles

The Pitts Lane

Croucheston Drove

High Road

High Road

Butt Lane

Flamstone Street

The Alley

Netton Street

Mill Lane

Stoke Farm

Bridge Road

Chapel Lane

The Cross

Croucheston Drove

Croucheston Drove

River Ebble

Croucheston

A 406

07

28

27

26

1 grid square represents 500 metres

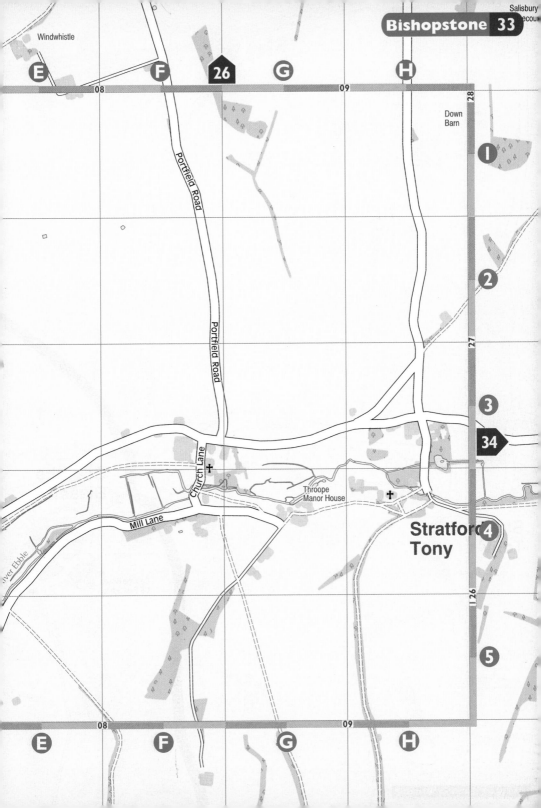

Salisbury
ecou

Windwhistle

E F **26** G H

08 09 28

Down
Barn

I

Portfield Road

2

27

Portfield Road

3

34

Church Lane

✝

Throope
Manor House

✝

**Stratford
Tony** **4**

Mill Lane

River Ebble

I 26

5

E F G H

08 09

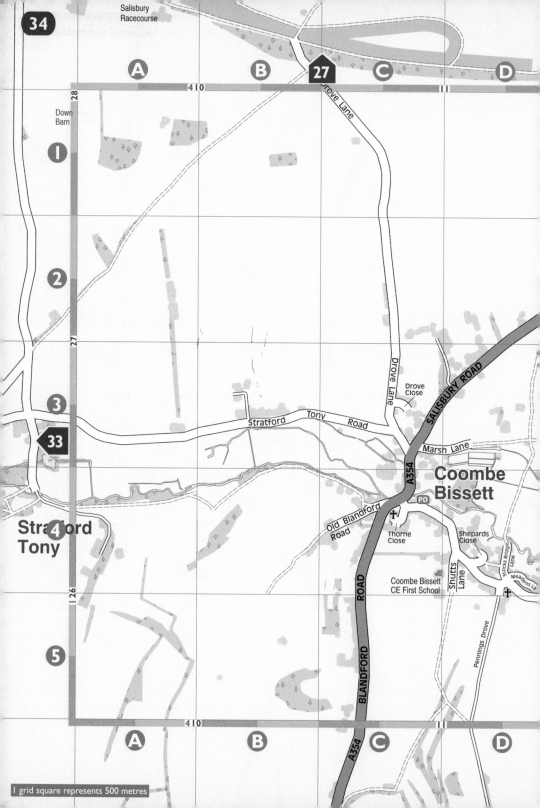

34

Salisbury
Racecourse

A   B   27   C   D

28   410

Down
Barn

1

Drove Lane

2

27

Drove Lane

Drove
Close

3

Stratford   Tony   Road

SALISBURY ROAD

33

Marsh Lane

A354

Coombe
Bissett

PO

Stratford
Tony

4

Old Blandford
Road

Thorne
Close

Shepards
Close

126

Stocks Bridge Lane

Shutts
Lane

Meadens La

Coombe Bissett
CE First School

5

BLANDFORD

ROAD

Pennings Drove

A354

410

A   B   C   D

1 grid square represents 500 metres

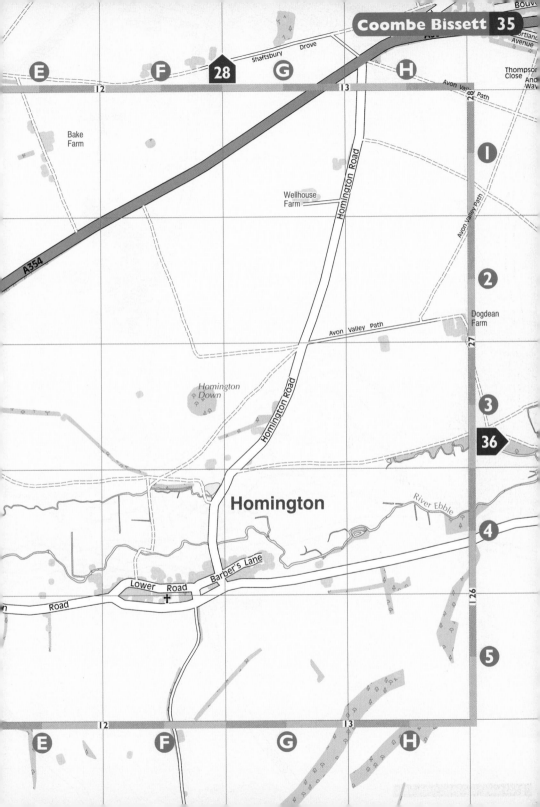

E   F   28   G   H

12

13

Shaftsbury   Drove

Avon Valley   Path

Bouv

Portland
Avenue

Thompson
Close
And
Way

I

Bake
Farm

Homington Road

Wellhouse
Farm

A354

Avon Valley Path

Avon Valley Path

2

27

Dogdean
Farm

Homington
Down

Homington Road

3

36

Homington

River Ebble

4

Lower   Road

Barber's Lane

Road

26

5

E   F   G   H

12

13

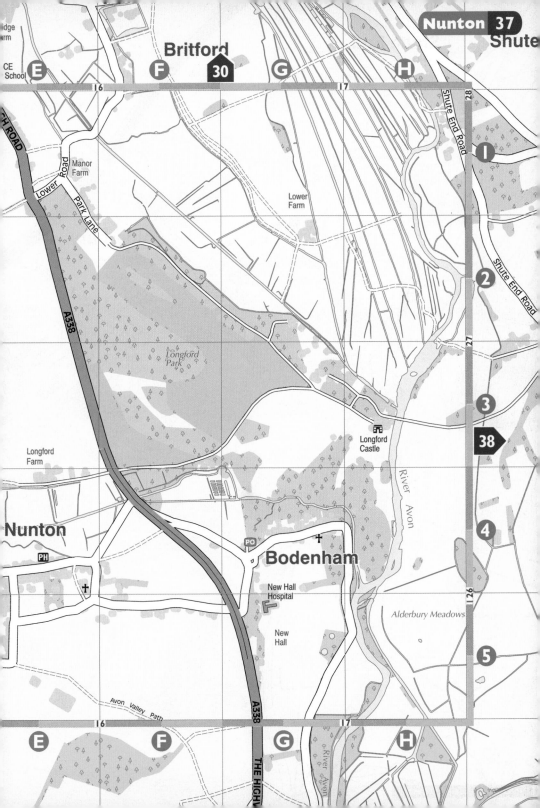

E   F   **30**   G   H

Britford

CE
School

16   17   28

H ROAD

Lower Road

Manor
Farm

Lower
Park Lane

Lower
Farm

I

A338

Shute End Road

2

27

Longford Park

Shute End Road

3

Longford Castle

River Avon

38

Longford Farm

Nunton

4

PO

† **Bodenham**

PH

†

New Hall Hospital

Alderbury Meadows

126

5

New Hall

Avon Valley Path

16   17

E   F   G   H

A338

THE HIGH

River Avon

E   F   G   H

20   Clarendon   Road   21   28

Whitehouse Farm

I

Long Drove

Common Plantation

Green Drove

Walden House

River Dunn

2

Butter   Furlong   Road

27

Whaddon Common

Crockford Road   Chapel Hill   Greenfields

3

Whistle Way

Grimstead   Church St

Road

Matrons Cots

A36

Grimstead Road

Kiln Close

West Grimstead

PO

Whaddon Bus Pk

4

Windwhistle Lane

Works

Alderbury Caravan & Camping Park

126

5

20   F   A36   21

E   F   G   H

Windwhistle Lane

A 22 417 B 18 C D

New Court Farm

Downton Industrial Estate

Batten Rd

David Hart Business Centre

1

Gravel

Barford

Cemete

†

Hamilton P

†

Church Hatch

The

Wick Lane

Long West

Long Cl

THE

BOROUGH

B3080

Mesh pond

Greenacres

Weeke Close

Joanna Cl

Elizabeth Cl

Marie Av

Downton CE Primary School

PO Cl

The Borough

Green La

South La

†

THE BOROUGH

PO

†

Wick

2

Catherine Crescent

Downton Secondary School

Surgery

Saxonhurst

Moot Lane

Moot Close

21

3

BREAMORE ROAD

A338

Moot Gardens

Squarey Close

Downlands Cl

Wynham Cl

Eastman Cl

Moot Lane

Cranbury Cl

River Avon

4

20

River Avon

5

N Charford Crossing

Hamp

Wilt

North Charford Manor House

Searchfield Farm

A 417 B C M Lane D

E   F   G   H

19   20   22

I

Muddyford Road

Templeman
Farm

Down House

Langford La

1

Sandy Lane

E HILL B3080

ownton

The
Business
Centre

The Row

PH

Grove   La   2

Chalk's
Cl

Rise Road

Bower's
Hill

Princes Hill   Pettircoat La

Redlynch

Appletree Rd

Morgan's   Rd

PO

Downton Hl

The Cl

Princes Cl

Kiln Lane

Morgan's
Vale

Orchard   Rd

Morgans Vale
& Woodfalls CE
Primary School

Apple Tree Cl

Bennett Cl

Vicarage Pk

Quavey Rd   3

Goog's

Primrose Lane

Morgans Vale Rd

Herbert
Rd

Chapel
Lane

von valley Path

Mitchells Cl

B3080

Vale

Castle
Woods

Road

Greens
Meade

Harthill
Drove

Slab Lane

Valley Cl

THE RIDGE

Church

Woodfalls

Elmfield

4   Lo

Kingsford Cl

Dairy Cl

PO

e Farm
e.

Highfield   Lane

Springfield Crs

Tinney's
Firs

Whiteshoot

Ltl Woodfalls Dr

Pineview
Cl

THE RIDGE

Tinneys

Avon

Lodge   Drove

Whiteshoot   Hill   5

Valley

North
Charford

FOREST RD

B3080

E   F   G   latchet
Green

H

Whiteshoot

Hatchet
Cl

Hale Lane

Carter's
Cl

Bohemia

FORE

Tethering Drove   Tetheri

Alderbury 38 C2	East Harnham 29 H4	Normanton 5 D5
Amesbury 11 E3	Elston 4 A2	North Charford 41 F5
Bemerton 23 E5	Ford 18 A5	Nunton 37 E4
Bemerton Heath 22 D2	Fugglestone 23 E1	Odstock 36 B4
Bishopdown 25 E3	Fugglestone Red 22 D1	The Pitts 32 D4
Bishopstone 32 C4	Fugglestone St Peter 22 C3	Porton 16 B3
Bodenham 37 G4	Gomeldon 16 B5	Quidhampton 22 C5
Britford 30 B5	Great Durnford 15 E2	Ratfyn 11 E1
Bulbridge 26 B1	Great Wishford 13 B3	Redlynch 41 H2
Bulford 8 C4	Homington 35 G4	Rollestone 4 B5
Bulford Camp 9 H4	Hurdcott 18 C4	Salisbury 2 D5
Burcombe 20 C5	Idmiston 16 D2	Serrington 12 B5
Churchfields 28 B1	Larkhill 6 C2	Shrewton 4 B4
Coombe Bissett 34 C4	Laverstock 25 F5	Shute End 31 E5
Ditchampton 21 H3	Morgan's Vale 41 F2	South Newton 13 D5
Downton 41 E2	Netherhampton 27 G2	Stapleford 12 C5
Durrington 7 G1	Netton 14 D4	Stoford 13 D2

Strangways ....
Stratford Sub Castle ....
Stratford Tony ....
Ugford ....
Upper Woodford ....
West Amesbury ....
West Grimstead ....
West Harnham ....
Whaddon ....
Wilton ....
Winterbourne Dauntsey ....
Winterbourne Earls ....
Winterbourne Gunner ....
Woodfalls ....

USING THE STREET INDEX

Street names are listed alphabetically. Each street name is followed by its postal town or area locality, the Postcode District, the page number, and the reference to the square in which the name is found.

Standard index entries are shown as follows:

Abbess Cl *AMSY* SP4 ....10 D4

Street names and selected addresses not shown on the map due to scale restrictions are shown in the index with an asterisk:

Aston Md *SAL* * SP1 ....24 D4

GENERAL ABBREVIATIONS

ACC ....ACCESS	E ....EAST	LDG ....LODGE	R ....RI
ALY ....ALLEY	EMB ....EMBANKMENT	LGT ....LIGHT	RBT ....ROUNDAB
AP ....APPROACH	EMBY ....EMBASSY	LK ....LOCK	RD ....R
AR ....ARCADE	ESP ....ESPLANADE	LKS ....LAKES	RDG ....R
ASS ....ASSOCIATION	EST ....ESTATE	LNDG ....LANDING	REP ....REPU
AV ....AVENUE	EX ....EXCHANGE	LTL ....LITTLE	RES ....RESERV
BCH ....BEACH	EXPY ....EXPRESSWAY	LWR ....LOWER	RFC ....RUGBY FOOTBALL C
BLDS ....BUILDINGS	EXT ....EXTENSION	MAG ....MAGISTRATE	RI ....
BND ....BEND	F/O ....FLYOVER	MAN ....MANSIONS	RP ....RA
BNK ....BANK	FC ....FOOTBALL CLUB	MD ....MEAD	RW ....R
BR ....BRIDGE	FK ....FORK	MDW ....MEADOWS	S ....SO
BRK ....BROOK	FLD ....FIELD	MEM ....MEMORIAL	SCH ....SCH
BTM ....BOTTOM	FLDS ....FIELDS	MKT ....MARKET	SE ....SOUTH E
BUS ....BUSINESS	FLS ....FALLS	MKTS ....MARKETS	SER ....SERVICE A
BVD ....BOULEVARD	FLS ....FLATS	ML ....MALL	SH ....SH
BY ....BYPASS	FM ....FARM	ML ....MILL	SHOP ....SHOPP
CATH ....CATHEDRAL	FT ....FORT	MNR ....MANOR	SKWY ....SKY
CEM ....CEMETERY	FWY ....FREEWAY	MS ....MEWS	SMT ....SUM
CEN ....CENTRE	FY ....FERRY	MSN ....MISSION	SOC ....SOC
CFT ....CROFT	GA ....GATE	MT ....MOUNT	SP ....S
CH ....CHURCH	GAL ....GALLERY	MTN ....MOUNTAIN	SPR ....SPR
CHA ....CHASE	GDN ....GARDEN	MTS ....MOUNTAINS	SQ ....SQU
CHYD ....CHURCHYARD	GDNS ....GARDENS	MUS ....MUSEUM	ST ....STR
CIR ....CIRCLE	GLD ....GLADE	MWY ....MOTORWAY	STN ....STAT
CIRC ....CIRCUS	GLN ....GLEN	N ....NORTH	STR ....STRE
CL ....CLOSE	GN ....GREEN	NE ....NORTH EAST	STRD ....STRA
CLFS ....CLIFFS	GND ....GROUND	NW ....NORTH WEST	SW ....SOUTH W
CMP ....CAMP	GRA ....GRANGE	O/P ....OVERPASS	TDG ....TRAD
CNR ....CORNER	GRG ....GARAGE	OFF ....OFFICE	TER ....TERR
CO ....COUNTY	GT ....GREAT	ORCH ....ORCHARD	THWY ....THROUGHW
COLL ....COLLEGE	GTWY ....GATEWAY	OV ....OVAL	TNL ....TUN
COM ....COMMON	GV ....GROVE	PAL ....PALACE	TOLL ....TOLL
COMM ....COMMISSION	HGR ....HIGHER	PAS ....PASSAGE	TPK ....TURNF
CON ....CONVENT	HL ....HILL	PAV ....PAVILION	TR ....TR
COT ....COTTAGE	HLS ....HILLS	PDE ....PARADE	TRL ....TF
COTS ....COTTAGES	HO ....HOUSE	PH ....PUBLIC HOUSE	TWR ....TO
CP ....CAPE	HOL ....HOLLOW	PK ....PARK	U/P ....UNDERP
CPS ....COPSE	HOSP ....HOSPITAL	PKWY ....PARKWAY	UNI ....UNIVERS
CR ....CREEK	HRB ....HARBOUR	PL ....PLACE	UPR ....UP
CREM ....CREMATORIUM	HTH ....HEATH	PLN ....PLAIN	V V
CRS ....CRESCENT	HTS ....HEIGHTS	PLNS ....PLAINS	VA ....VAL
CSWY ....CAUSEWAY	HVN ....HAVEN	PLZ ....PLAZA	VIAD ....VIAD
CT ....COURT	HWY ....HIGHWAY	POL ....POLICE STATION	VIL V
CTRL ....CENTRAL	IMP ....IMPERIAL	PR ....PRINCE	VIS V
CTS ....COURTS	IN ....INLET	PREC ....PRECINCT	VLG VILL
CTYD ....COURTYARD	IND EST ....INDUSTRIAL ESTATE	PREP ....PREPARATORY	VLS VIL
CUTT ....CUTTINGS	INF ....INFIRMARY	PRIM ....PRIMARY	VW V
CV ....COVE	INFO ....INFORMATION	PROM ....PROMENADE	W ....W
CYN ....CANYON	INT ....INTERCHANGE	PRS ....PRINCESS	WD ....WC
DEPT ....DEPARTMENT	IS ....ISLAND	PRT ....PORT	WHF ....WH
DL ....DALE	JCT ....JUNCTION	PT ....POINT	WK ....WA
DM ....DAM	JTY ....JETTY	PTH ....PATH	WKS ....WA
DR ....DRIVE	KG ....KING	PZ ....PIAZZA	WLS ....WA
DRO ....DROVE	KNL ....KNOLL	QD ....QUADRANT	WY V
DRY ....DRIVEWAY	L ....LAKE	QU ....QUEEN	YD ....YD
DWGS ....DWELLINGS	LA ....LANE	QY ....QUAY	YHA ....YOUTH HOS

POSTCODE TOWNS AND AREA ABBREVIATIONS

AMSY ....Amesbury	RSAL ....Rural Salisbury	RSALW/SHRW ....Rural Salisbury west/ Shrewton	SAL ....Salis
FBDG ....Fordingbridge			SALW/WIL ....Salisbury west/W

A

ess Cl AMSY SP4	10 D4
ey Cl RSALW/SHRW SP3	4 A4
ot Rd SAL SP1	24 D3
son Sq AMSY SP4	7 H2
aide Cl AMSY SP4	9 G4
brook Cl AMSY SP4	10 D2
brooke Rd AMSY SP4	6 B3
any Rd SAL SP1	3 G2
vorth Dr SAL SP1	24 D2
andra Cl SALW/WIL SP2	23 F4
dry Rd AMSY SP4	19 F2
Alley RSAL SP5	32 C5
gton Wy AMSY SP4	11 F4
sbury Rd AMSY SP4	11 G3
SALW/SHRW SP3	4 A4
ient Wy SALW/WIL SP2	29 C5
erson Rd SAL SP1	24 D3
rew Cl AMSY SP4	7 H2
rews Wy SALW/WIL SP2	29 E5
ler Rd SALW/WIL SP2	23 E2
e Crs AMSY SP4	7 H2
etts Cl AMSY SP4	11 E2
robus Rd AMSY SP4	10 D3
stle Wy SAL SP1	24 D2
eshaw Wy SAL SP1	25 E2
e Tree Cl RSAL SP5	41 G2
gon Cl AMSY SP4	11 E2
ners Ct SALW/WIL SP2	3 F2
itage Sq AMSY SP4	6 A3
Crs SAL SP1	24 D2
field Rd SALW/WIL SP2	2 A3
ands SAL SP1	25 E1
eigh Cl SALW/WIL SP2	13 D4
ey Rd SALW/WIL SP2	2 D2
ey Wk AMSY SP4	11 F4
si Rd SAL SP1	24 B2
n Md SAL * SP1	24 D4
wood Rd SAL SP1	24 B4
kland Rd AMSY SP4	9 G2
ralian Av SALW/WIL SP2	23 G5
Avenue AMSY SP4	7 H2
SALW/WIL SP2	16 C3
L SP1	3 J4
L SP1	25 E5
LW/WIL SP2	22 C2
n Ap SALW/WIL SP2	2 E4
n Br SALW/WIL SP2	23 G1
ndown Rd AMSY SP4	8 A2
n Dr RSAL SP5	38 D3
n Mdw AMSY SP4	14 B5
n Rd AMSY SP4	9 G3
nstoke Cl AMSY SP4	10 D4
n Ter SALW/WIL SP2	2 D2
n Valley Pth RSAL SP5	41 G5
LW/WIL SP2	29 E4
eswade Rd SALW/WIL SP2	29 F4
shire Cl SALW/WIL SP2	23 E2

B

hdad Rd AMSY SP4	9 G2
moral Rd SAL SP1	24 C3
er's La RSAL SP5	35 F4
ford La RSAL SP5	40 D1
nards Hill Dr SALW/WIL SP2	23 F3
nes Wallis Cl AMSY SP4	11 G3
rington Rd SAL SP1	24 D3
tlett Rd SAL SP1	24 C4
ten Rd RSAL SP5	40 B1
vdsey Rd AMSY SP4	11 F4
con Cl AMSY SP4	11 E2
con Hill Rd AMSY SP4	9 H2
atrice Rd SAL SP1	24 B3
uchamp Dr AMSY SP4	11 F3
ulieu Rd AMSY SP4	11 E4
umont Wy AMSY SP4	11 F3
ford Rd SALW/WIL SP2	2 B2
win AMSY * SP4	7 H2
win St SAL SP1	3 G5
ch Cl AMSY SP4	16 C3
chcroft Rd SAL SP1	30 A1
Beeches SAL SP1	3 J6
amy La SAL SP1	3 J4
e Vue Pl SAL * SP1	3 F3
e Vue Rd SAL SP1	3 F3
AMSY SP4	6 C1
gal Rd AMSY SP4	9 F3
nett Cl RSAL SP5	41 G3
kshire Rd SALW/WIL SP2	2 A7
wick Br RSALW/SHRW SP3	12 C5
wick Rd RSALW/SHRW SP3	12 C5

Beyer Rd AMSY SP4	11 E4
Biddulph Rd AMSY SP4	7 E2
Bingham Rd AMSY SP4	6 B2
SAL SP1	24 D3
Birchwood Dr AMSY SP4	8 A2
Bishopdown Rd SAL SP1	24 D3
Bishops Dr SALW/WIL SP2	29 E4
Bishops Md AMSY SP4	25 F3
Bishop's Wk SAL SP1	3 F6
Blackbarn Rd AMSY SP4	17 G4
Blackcross Rd AMSY SP4	11 E4
Blackfriars Wy SAL SP1	3 C6
Black Horse La AMSY SP4	18 C4
Blakey Rd SAL SP1	3 J6
Blandford Rd RSAL SP5	34 C5
Blue Boar Rw SAL SP1	3 F5
Blyth Wy SAL SP1	25 E3
Bonaker Cl AMSY SP4	16 C3
Bond St AMSY SP4	9 E4
Bonnewe Ri AMSY SP4	11 F3
The Borough RSAL SP5	40 B2
Boscombe Rd AMSY SP4	11 E3
Bouchers Wy SALW/WIL SP2	29 F5
Boundary Rd SAL SP1	25 F5
Bourne Av SAL SP1	3 J2
Bourne Cl AMSY SP4	16 C3
SAL SP1	30 A2
Bourne Gdns AMSY SP4	16 C2
Bourne Hl SAL SP1	3 G3
Bourne Valley Cl AMSY SP4	16 D4
Bourne Wy SAL SP1	30 A3
Bouverie Av SALW/WIL SP2	29 E4
Bouverie Av South	
SALW/WIL SP2	29 E5
Bouverie Cl SALW/WIL SP2	29 E4
Bowdich Rd AMSY SP4	8 A1
Bower Gdns SAL SP1	3 K6
Bower Hill Rd SAL SP1	3 J1
Bowers Hl RSAL SP5	41 H2
Bowes Lyon Ct AMSY SP4	23 G4
Brackenbury Rd AMSY SP4	6 A1
Bracken Cl RSAL SP5	38 C2
Braemar Ri SAL SP1	3 C3
The Brambles SAL SP1	3 J2
Bramley Wy AMSY SP4	11 E3
Breamore Rd RSAL SP5	40 A3
Brewery La SAL * SP1	3 G5
Brick La SALW/WIL SP2	23 F5
Bridge Rd RSAL SP5	32 C5
Bridge St SALW/WIL SP2	2 E5
Brind Rd AMSY SP4	6 D1
Brisbane Gdns AMSY SP4	9 G4
Britford La SALW/WIL SP2	29 G4
Britford La West SALW/WIL SP2	29 F4
Broadfield Rd AMSY SP4	19 G1
Broadfields SAL SP1	19 G1
Broadlands Cl SAL SP1	24 C3
Brocks Orch RSALW/SHRW SP3	4 A5
Brown St SAL SP1	3 G5
Brunel Rd AMSY SP4	28 C2
Bulbridge Rd SALW/WIL SP2	26 C1
Bulford Droveway AMSY SP4	8 C3
Bulford Hl AMSY SP4	8 A3
Bulford Rd AMSY SP4	7 H1
AMSY SP4	8 B3
Bungalow Pk AMSY * SP4	11 E2
Burcombe La SALW/WIL SP2	21 G5
Burford Av SALW/WIL SP2	29 G4
Burford Rd SALW/WIL SP2	29 G4
Burgess Gn SAL SP1	24 D3
Burnet Wy SAL SP1	25 E3
Burwood Cl AMSY SP4	11 G3
Bury Rd RSALW/SHRW SP3	12 B4
Butcher Rw SAL * SP1	3 F5
Butler Cl SALW/WIL SP2	29 C4
Butterfield Dr AMSY SP4	11 F4
Butter Furlong Rd RSAL SP5	39 G2
Butt La RSAL SP5	32 C5
The Butts RSALW/SHRW SP3	4 A3
Butts Hl RSALW/SHRW SP3	12 C4
Butts Rd SAL SP1	2 E1
Byways SAL SP1	3 J5

C

Cadnam Crs AMSY SP4	11 G4
Cambridge Rd SAL SP1	24 C4
Camilla Cl AMSY SP4	8 B3
Campbell Rd SAL SP1	3 H1
Canadian Av SALW/WIL SP2	23 G5
Canal La RSAL SP5	38 D3
Canalside RSAL SP5	38 D3
Canberra Dr AMSY SP4	9 G4
Canterbury Cl AMSY SP4	11 F3
Capulet Rd SAL SP1	24 A3
Carleton Pl AMSY SP4	10 C2

Carlton Cl AMSY SP4	11 F3
Carmelite Wy SAL SP1	3 G7
Carpenter Dr AMSY SP4	11 F3
Carrion Pond Dro	
SALW/WIL SP2	28 C3
Castle Keep SAL SP1	23 H3
SALW/WIL SP2	22 A4
Castle La RSAL SP5	38 D4
SALW/WIL SP2	22 A4
Castle Rd SAL SP1	24 B2
Castle Rbt SAL SP1	3 F1
Castle St SAL SP1	3 F3
Castle Woods RSAL SP5	41 G3
Cathedral Ct SAL SP1	3 F6
Cathedral Views	
SALW/WIL * SP2	2 E5
Catherine Ct SAL SP1	3 F5
Catherine Crs RSAL SP5	40 A2
Catherine St SAL SP1	3 F5
Cator Rd AMSY SP4	6 B2
Cecil Av SALW/WIL SP2	29 F5
Cecil Ter SALW/WIL SP2	28 C1
Cedar Cl SALW/WIL SP2	23 E3
The Centre AMSY SP4	10 C2
Centurion Cl SALW/WIL SP2	23 G5
Chain Dro RSALW/SHRW SP3	12 C5
Chain Hl RSALW/SHRW SP3	12 C5
Chalk Hl RSALW/SHRW SP3	4 A5
Chalk's Cl RSAL SP5	41 G2
Chambers Av AMSY SP4	11 E4
Chancery Cl SALW/WIL SP2	2 A2
Chantry Cl AMSY * SP4	7 H1
Chantry Rd SALW/WIL SP2	26 D1
Chants La RSALW/SHRW SP3	4 A5
Chapel Hl RSAL SP5	39 G3
Chapel La RSAL SP5	41 H3
RSALW/SHRW SP3	4 A4
RSALW/SHRW SP3	12 C5
Chapel Pl SALW/WIL SP2	2 E4
Charles Rd AMSY SP4	7 H2
Charles St SAL SP1	2 C3
Charnwood Rd SALW/WIL SP2	2 A3
Charter Ct SAL * SP1	3 G5
Chatham St SAL SP1	24 A3
Cheese Market SAL SP1	3 F5
Cherry Cl SALW/WIL SP2	28 C1
Cherry Orchard La	
SALW/WIL SP2	28 C1
Cherry Tree Wy AMSY SP4	11 E3
Cheshire Cl SALW/WIL SP2	23 F3
Chesterfield Cl AMSY SP4	11 G3
Chestnut Cl SAL SP1	25 E4
Cheverell Av SAL SP1	24 D4
Chichester Cl SALW/WIL SP2	29 G4
Chine Rd AMSY SP4	14 A3
Chipper La SAL SP1	3 F4
Chiselbury Gv SALW/WIL SP2	29 F4
Choristers Sq SALW/WIL SP2	2 E6
Christie Miller Rd SALW/WIL SP2	2 A1
Christopher Cl SALW/WIL SP2	29 E5
Churchfields Rd SALW/WIL SP2	2 C3
Church Furlong	
RSALW/SHRW SP3	12 B5
Church Hatch RSAL SP5	40 D1
Churchill Av AMSY SP4	8 C3
Churchill Ct SALW/WIL SP2	22 A4
Churchill Wy East SAL SP1	3 H4
Churchill Wy North SAL SP1	3 F3
Churchill Wy South SAL SP1	29 G3
Churchill Wy West	
SALW/WIL SP2	2 E2
Church La AMSY SP4	8 B3
AMSY SP4	10 C3
RSAL SP5	30 B5
RSAL SP5	33 F4
SALW/WIL SP2	23 F5
Church Pk AMSY * SP4	7 H1
Church Rd AMSY SP4	17 G1
SAL SP1	25 F4
Church St AMSY SP4	7 H1
AMSY SP4	10 C3
RSAL SP5	39 H3
SAL SP1	3 H6
Chur St AMSY SP4	9 F3
Clarence Ct SAL * SP1	3 G4
Clarendon Rd RSAL SP5	30 C4
RSAL SP5	38 C2
RSAL SP5	39 F1
SAL SP1	3 J4
Clarendon Wy RSAL SP5	31 E1
SAL SP1	2 E7
SALW/WIL SP2	29 F4
Clayton Rd AMSY SP4	8 C3
The Cleeves RSALW/SHRW SP3	20 A4
Clifton Cl SALW/WIL SP2	2 C2
Clifton Rw SALW/WIL * SP2	2 D3
The Close AMSY SP4	18 A4
RSAL SP5	41 G2

SAL SP1	2 E6
Club Rd AMSY SP4	9 F2
Coach House Ms AMSY SP4	10 D3
Cocks Cl AMSY SP4	6 B2
Cold Harbour AMSY SP4	10 D2
Coldharbour La SALW/WIL SP2	2 C1
College Rd AMSY SP4	7 H1
College St SAL SP1	3 G2
Colquhoun Rd AMSY SP4	7 E3
Coltsfoot Cl AMSY SP4	11 E3
The Common RSALW/SHRW SP3	4 A5
Congreve Rd AMSY SP4	6 B2
Coniston Cl AMSY SP4	11 G3
Constable Wy SALW/WIL SP2	2 B7
Cooks Cl SALW/WIL SP2	23 E2
Coombe Rd SALW/WIL SP2	29 E5
Coopers Cl AMSY SP4	10 D2
The Copse RSAL SP5	38 C3
Cornwall Rd SAL SP1	24 B4
Coronation Rd AMSY SP4	7 H2
SALW/WIL SP2	23 G4
Countess Rd AMSY SP4	10 C2
Courtwood Cl SAL SP1	3 J5
Cow La SAL SP1	3 K2
Cranbury Cl RSAL SP5	40 C3
Cranebridge Rd SALW/WIL SP2	2 E5
Crane St SAL SP1	2 E5
The Crescent AMSY SP4	9 H2
SAL * SP1	3 H4
SALW/WIL SP2	21 G5
Crescent Rd AMSY SP4	8 B4
Crestmount Dr SALW/WIL SP2	23 F4
Crockford Rd RSAL SP5	39 F3
The Croft RSAL SP5	32 C5
Cross Keys Chequer SAL SP1	3 G5
Crouchestone Dro RSAL SP5	32 B4
Crow La SAL SP1	22 A4
Crown Cl SALW/WIL SP2	23 G4
The Crusades SAL SP1	24 D2
Culver St SAL SP1	3 H5
Cygnet Dr AMSY SP4	8 A3

D

Dairy Cl RSAL SP5	41 G4
Dairy Meadow La SAL SP1	30 A3
Dalewood Ri SAL SP1	25 F5
Darrell Rd AMSY SP4	11 E2
Darwin Cl AMSY SP4	9 G4
Dawbeney Dr AMSY SP4	11 F3
Denison Ri SAL SP1	24 D4
De Vaux Pl SAL SP1	29 F3
Devereux Rd AMSY SP4	10 D3
Devizes Rd SALW/WIL SP2	2 B2
Devonshire Rd SAL SP1	24 B4
Dew's Rd SAL SP1	2 D4
Diddledown Rd AMSY SP4	11 E4
Dolphin St SAL SP1	3 H5
Donaldson Rd SAL SP1	3 F1
Dorset Cl AMSY SP4	8 C3
Dorset Rd SAL SP1	24 C4
Double Hedges AMSY SP4	8 D4
Douglas Brown's Wk AMSY SP4	6 B3
Douglas Haig Rd SAL SP1	2 E1
Down Barn Cl AMSY SP4	16 A5
Downlands Cl RSAL SP5	40 C3
Downland Wy AMSY SP4	7 G2
Downleaze AMSY SP4	7 H1
Downsway SAL SP1	24 C2
Downton Hl RSAL SP5	41 F2
Downton Rd SALW/WIL SP2	29 G4
Down View Rd SAL SP1	25 F5
The Drove AMSY SP4	10 D2
Drove Cl RSAL SP5	34 C3
Drove La RSAL SP5	27 F5
Dryden Cl SALW/WIL SP2	29 G5
Duck La RSALW/SHRW SP3	20 A4
	25 E5
Duck St RSALW/SHRW SP3	12 C1
Duke's Wy AMSY SP4	8 C3
Dunley Wy SAL SP1	24 D2

E

Eagle Fld SALW/WIL SP2	23 G3
Earls Cl AMSY SP4	11 G4
Earls Court Rd AMSY SP4	10 D3
Earl's Ri AMSY SP4	18 D3
East Gomeldon Rd AMSY SP4	16 C5
Eastman Cl RSAL SP5	40 D3
East St SALW/WIL SP2	2 D4
Edgam Pl SALW/WIL SP2	22 C4
Edison Rd SALW/WIL SP2	2 A5

Edwards Rd *AMSY* SP4 ....10 D3
Egerton Pl *SALW/WIL* * SP2 ....2 C3
Elizabeth Cl *RSAL* SP5 ....40 A2
Elizabeth Rd *AMSY* SP4................7 H2
   SALW/WIL SP2 ....21 G2
Elliott Gn *AMSY* SP4...................19 F1
Elm Cl *SAL* SP1 ....25 E4
Elmfield Cl *RSAL* SP5 ....41 G4
Elm Gv *SAL* SP1...........................3 H4
Elm Grove Pl *SAL* SP1 ....3 J4
Elm Grove Rd *SAL* SP1 ....3 H4
Empire Rd *SALW/WIL* SP2 ....23 F5
Endless St *SAL* SP1 ....3 F3
Essex Sq *SAL* SP1 ....28 C4
Estcourt Rd *SAL* SP1 ....3 H3
Eveque Ct *SAL* SP1 ....22 D5
Evergreen Wy *AMSY* SP4 ....11 E4
Exeter St *SAL* SP1........................3 G7
Eyres Dr *RSAL* SP5 ....38 D3
Eyres Wy *SAL* SP1 ....3 H6

F

Fairfax Cl *AMSY* SP4 ....10 C2
Fairfield Rd *SAL* SP1 ....24 B3
Fairview Rd *SAL* SP1 ....3 J3
Fair View Rd *SALW/WIL* SP2 ....22 B3
Falconsway *SALW/WIL* SP2 ....29 F5
Faraday Rd *SALW/WIL* SP2 ....2 A4
Fargo Cl *AMSY* SP4......................7 F4
Fargo Rd *AMSY* SP4......................6 B3
Farley Rd *SAL* SP1.......................3 K7
Farm La *SAL* SP1 ....2 A4
Far View Rd *RSALW/SHRW* SP3 ....4 B3
Festival Av *SALW/WIL* SP2 ....23 F4
Feversham Rd *SAL* SP1 ....24 B4
Figsbury Rdg *AMSY* SP4 ....19 G2
Figsbury Rd *AMSY* SP4 ....19 E3
Finchley Rd *SALW/WIL* SP2............2 A3
Finnis Rd *AMSY* SP4....................10 D3
Firs Rd *RSAL* SP5 ....38 D3
Fisherton Island *SALW/WIL* SP2 .....2 C4
Fisherton St *SALW/WIL* SP2............2 D4
Fish Rw *SAL* * SP1 ....3 F5
Flamstone St *RSAL* SP5..............32 B5
Flit Cft *AMSY* SP4.......................11 E4
Flower La *AMSY* SP4 ....10 C3
Folkestone Rd *SALW/WIL* SP2 .....29 E4
Folly Cl *SALW/WIL* SP2 ....29 E5
Folly La *RSAL* SP5 ....38 B2
   SALW/WIL SP2 ....23 G5
Folly Vw *SALW/WIL* SP2 ....29 F3
Foot's Hl *SALW/WIL* SP2 ....22 D4
Forest Rd *FBDG* SP6....................41 G5
Forge Cl *SALW/WIL* SP2 ....13 D4
Fosters Bushes *AMSY* SP4 ....11 F3
Fotherby Crs *SAL* SP1 ....24 D3
Foundry Rd *RSAL* SP5.................41 G2
Fowler's Hl *SAL* SP1 ....3 J6
Fowler's Rd *SAL* SP1 ....3 H5
Francis Wy *SALW/WIL* SP2 ....29 E5
Friar's Orch *SAL* SP1 ....3 G6
The Friary *SAL* SP1.......................3 G6
Friary La *SAL* SP1 ....3 G7
Fugglestone *SALW/WIL* SP2........22 B3
Furlong Crs *RSALW/SHRW* SP3 ....4 B3
Furlong Wy *RSALW/SHRW* SP3 ....4 A3
Fyfield Cl *SAL* SP1 ....25 E2

G

Gainsborough Cl *SALW/WIL* SP2 ..23 F4
Gallipoli Rd *AMSY* SP4.................9 H3
Gardiner Rd *AMSY* SP4.................6 B3
Gas La *SALW/WIL* SP2 ....2 C3
Gaters La *AMSY* SP4...................18 D2
Gauntlet Rd *AMSY* SP4 ....10 D2
Gawthorne Dr *SALW/WIL* SP2 .....29 E4
Gaza Rd *AMSY* SP4......................9 G2
Geneville Ri *AMSY* SP4 ....11 E3
George St *SALW/WIL* SP2..............2 D2
George St South *SALW/WIL* SP2 ....2 D3
Gibbs Cl *SAL* SP1.......................24 D2
Gigant St *SAL* SP1........................3 G5
Gilbert Wy *SAL* SP1 ....24 D3
Glebe Rd *AMSY* SP4 ....7 H1
Glendale Crs *SAL* SP1 ....30 A2
Glendale Rd *AMSY* SP4................8 A2
Glenmore Rd *SAL* SP1 ....24 D4
Glover Rd *AMSY* SP4....................6 D1
Glyndebourne Cl *SALW/WIL* SP2 ..23 F4
Godley Rd *SALW/WIL* SP2 ....29 F4
Gomeldon Rd *AMSY* SP4 ....19 F1
Goodbody Rd *AMSY* SP4 ....7 E3

Gore Rd *AMSY* SP4......................6 B2
Gorringe Rd *SALW/WIL* SP2 ....28 C1
Grace Cl *SALW/WIL* SP2 ....23 E2
Gramshaw Rd *SALW/WIL* SP2 .....23 G5
Grange Gdns *SAL* SP1 ....3 J1
Grasmere Cl *SALW/WIL* SP2 ....29 E4
Gravel Cl *RSAL* SP5 ....40 B1
The Green *RSAL* SP5 ....38 B2
   SAL SP1..............................25 E5
Greenacres *SAL* SP5 ....40 A2
The Greencroft *SAL* * SP1............3 H4
Greencroft St *SAL* SP1..................3 G3
Green Dro *RSAL* SP5 ....39 G1
Greenfields *RSAL* SP5 ....39 H3
Greenlands Cl *AMSY* SP4.............7 H2
Green La *AMSY* SP4 ....18 A5
   RSAL SP5.............................40 C1
Greenlane Cl *AMSY* SP4.............25 E1
Green's Ct *SAL* SP1 ....3 G6
Greens Meade *RSAL* SP5 ....41 G3
Greenwood Av *SAL* SP1 ....30 A1
Greyfriars Cl *SAL* SP1....................3 G7
Greyhound La *SALW/WIL* * SP2 ...22 A4
Griffins Ct *SALW/WIL* SP2 ....2 E4
Grimstead Rd *RSAL* SP5 ....39 E4
Groveley Rd *RSALW/SHRW* SP3 ..20 A4
Grovely Vw *SALW/WIL* SP2 ....26 C1
Guilder La *SAL* SP1 ....3 H4
Gunner St *AMSY* SP4 ....9 E4

H

Hackthorne Rd *AMSY* SP4 ....7 G1
Hadrians Cl *SALW/WIL* SP2 ....28 B1
Haig Rd *AMSY* SP4.......................9 F3
Hallum Cl *SAL* SP1 ....25 E3
The Ham *AMSY* SP4.....................8 A1
Hamilton Cl *SALW/WIL* SP2 ....11 F3
Hamilton Pk *RSAL* SP5 ....40 D1
Hamilton Rd *SAL* SP1....................3 F2
Hampshire Cl *AMSY* SP4...............8 C3
Hampton Cl *SALW/WIL* SP2 ....22 C5
Harcourt Ter *SALW/WIL* SP2 ....2 D5
The Hardings *SALW/WIL* * SP2 ......2 C3
Hare Warren Cl *SALW/WIL* SP2 ...26 D1
Harnham Br *SALW/WIL* SP2 ....29 G3
Harnham Rd *SALW/WIL* SP2 ....28 D3
Harnwood Rd *SALW/WIL* SP2 ......28 D5
Harper Rd *SALW/WIL* SP2 ....23 G5
Harrington Dr *AMSY* SP4 ....9 F3
Harthill Dro *RSAL* SP5.................41 H4
Hartington Rd *SALW/WIL* SP2 ....2 C2
Hartley Wy *SAL* SP1 ....25 E2
Harvard Cl *SALW/WIL* SP2 ....29 E5
Harvard Wy *AMSY* SP4 ....11 F4
Harvest La *RSAL* SP5 ....32 D5
Hatches La *SAL* SP1 ....30 A3
Hathaway Cl *SAL* SP1 ....24 A3
Hawksridge *SALW/WIL* SP2 ....29 F5
Hawthorn Cl *SALW/WIL* SP2 ....2 C3
Haywain *AMSY* SP4 ....10 D3
Hazel Cl *SALW/WIL* SP2 ....23 E4
Headquarters Rd *AMSY* SP4 ....9 C4
Heath Rd *SALW/WIL* SP2 ....23 G3
Heath Sq *AMSY* SP4 ....6 B3
Helena Ter *SAL* * SP1 ....3 H3
Herbert Rd *RSAL* SP5 ....41 G3
   SALW/WIL SP2 ....23 F4
Heronswood *SALW/WIL* SP2 ....29 F5
Heron Wk *AMSY* SP4 ....8 A2
Heyford Cl *AMSY* SP4 ....11 G3
Highbury Av *SALW/WIL* SP2 ....2 A2
Highbury Cl *SALW/WIL* SP2...........2 A1
Highfield Cl *RSALW/SHRW* SP3 ....4 B4
Highfield La *RSAL* SP5................41 G4
Highfield Ri *RSALW/SHRW* SP3 ....4 B4
Highfield Rd *SALW/WIL* SP2 ....10 D3
   SALW/WIL SP2 ....2 B2
Highlands Rd *SALW/WIL* SP2 ......29 F4
Highland Vw *SALW/WIL* SP2 ....13 C4
High Rd *RSAL* SP5......................32 A5
   RSAL SP5.............................37 E1
High St *SALW/WIL* SP2..................7 H1
   AMSY SP4..............................8 A3
   AMSY SP4............................10 C2
   AMSY SP4............................16 C4
   RSAL SP5.............................38 B2
   RSALW/SHRW SP3..................4 A4
   RSALW/SHRW SP3................12 C1
   SAL SP1.................................1 F5
Hill Rd *SAL* SP1..........................25 F5
Hill Side *RSALW/SHRW* SP3 ....12 C4
Hillside Dr *AMSY* SP4 ....19 G1
Hillside Rd *SALW/WIL* SP2 ....13 D4
Hilltop Wy *SAL* SP1 ....24 B2
Hillview Cl *AMSY* SP4..................10 D2

Hill View Rd *SAL* SP1 ....3 H4
Hinde's Meadow
   RSALW/SHRW SP3..................4 B2
Hoadley Gn *SAL* SP1 ....25 E3
Holders Rd *AMSY* SP4 ....11 E2
The Hollow *RSALW/SHRW* SP3 .....4 A3
The Hollows *SALW/WIL* SP2 ....21 G3
Hollows Cl *SALW/WIL* SP2 ....29 E4
Home Farm Rd *SALW/WIL* SP2 ....26 D1
Homington Rd *RSAL* SP5 ....34 D5
Horne Rd *AMSY* SP4 ....9 E2
Horse Barrow *AMSY* SP4 ....19 F1
Howard-Vyse Rd *AMSY* SP4.........6 B2
Hubert Hamilton Rd *AMSY* SP4 ....9 F3
Hudson Rd *AMSY* SP4 ....11 E2
   AMSY SP4............................24 A4
Hulse Rd *SAL* SP1........................2 E1
Hurdcott La *AMSY* SP4 ....18 C4
Hurley Cl *AMSY* SP4....................11 F3

I

Idmiston Rd *AMSY* SP4 ....16 D3
Imber Av *AMSY* SP4....................11 F4
India Av *SALW/WIL* SP2 ....2 A1
Ivy Pl *SALW/WIL* * SP2 ....3 F3
Ivy St *SAL* SP1............................3 G5

J

Jaggard Vw *AMSY* SP4 ....11 E3
James Rd *AMSY* SP4 ....11 E2
James St *SALW/WIL* SP2...............2 D3
Javelin Cl *AMSY* SP4...................11 F3
Jewell Cl *SAL* SP1 ....25 E3
Joanna Cl *RSAL* SP5 ....40 A2
John French Wy *AMSY* SP4 ....8 C3
John Gay Rd *AMSY* SP4 ....10 D3
Jubilee Ct *SALW/WIL* SP2 ....2 D2
Jubilee Hl *AMSY* SP4 ....9 F4
Junction Rd *RSAL* SP5 ....38 D2
Juniper Dr *SAL* SP1 ....24 B2

K

Kandy Rd *AMSY* SP4 ....9 F3
Kashmir Rd *AMSY* SP4 ....9 F3
Kelsey Rd *SAL* SP1 ....3 H4
Kensington Rd *SALW/WIL* SP2 ....2 C1
Kent Rd *SALW/WIL* SP2 ....28 D3
Kickdom Cl *AMSY* SP4 ....11 F4
Kiln Cl *RSAL* SP5 ....39 E4
Kiln La *RSAL* SP5.......................41 H2
Kimpton Av *SAL* SP1 ....25 E2
Kingfisher Cl *SALW/WIL* SP2........11 E3
Kingfisher Dr *AMSY* SP4................8 A2
Kingsbourne Cl *AMSY* SP4 ....11 E3
Kingsbury Sq *SALW/WIL* SP2 ......22 A4
Kingsford Cl *RSAL* SP5...............41 G4
Kings Ga *SALW/WIL* SP2 ....22 B3
Kingsland Rd *SALW/WIL* SP2 ....2 C2
Kingsmead *SALW/WIL* SP2 ....13 C3
King's Rd *SAL* SP1........................3 F2
King St *SALW/WIL* SP2 ....22 A3
Kingsway *SALW/WIL* SP2 ....22 A3
Kitchener Rd *AMSY* SP4 ....10 D2
Kivel Ct *SALW/WIL* SP2 ....2 E2
Kiwi Rd *AMSY* SP4 ....9 H2

L

Ladysmith *AMSY* SP4 ....19 G1
Ladysmith Rd *SALW/WIL* SP2 ......23 G4
Lane's Cl *AMSY* SP4 ....11 E2
Lanfear Cl *AMSY* SP4 ....11 E2
Langford La *RSAL* SP5................41 G1
Langford Rd *SALW/WIL* SP2 ....13 B2
Larkhill Rd *AMSY* SP4....................7 H2
Laverstock Pk *SAL* SP1 ....25 E5
Laverstock Pk West *SAL* SP1 ......25 E5
Laverstock Rd *SAL* SP1 ....3 J5
Lawrence Cl *AMSY* SP4 ....11 E4
Lawrence Gn *SALW/WIL* * SP2 ......2 C2
Lawrence Rd *AMSY* SP4................6 C2
Lawson Rd *AMSY* SP4 ....7 E3
The Leaze *AMSY* SP4....................8 C3
Ledger Hill Cl *AMSY* SP4 ....8 B3
Lees Ct *SALW/WIL* SP2 ....2 C2
Leonard Cheshire Cl *AMSY* SP4 ..11 F4
Lightfoot Rd *AMSY* SP4.................6 C3

Lightning Rd *AMSY* * SP4 ....
Light's La *RSAL* SP5 ....
Lily Wk *AMSY* SP4 ....
Lime Kiln Wy *SALW/WIL* SP2 ....
The Limes *AMSY* SP4 ....
Linden Cl *SAL* SP1 ....
Lindford Rd *SAL* SP1 ....
Link Wy *SAL* SP1 ....
Linnetsdene *SALW/WIL* SP2 ....
Little Woodfalls Dr *RSAL* SP5 ......
Lock's La *SALW/WIL* SP2 ....
Lode Hl *RSAL* SP5 ....
Lodge Dro *RSAL* SP5 ....
Londonderry Gdns *AMSY* SP4 .....
London Rd *SAL* SP1 ....
   RSALW/SHRW SP3..................
   SAL SP1..............................
Long Cl *RSAL* SP5 ....
Long Cl West *RSAL* SP5 ....
Long Dro *RSAL* SP5 ....
Longfield Cl *AMSY* SP4 ....
Longhill Dr *SALW/WIL* SP2 ....
Longland *SALW/WIL* SP2 ....
Lords Cft *AMSY* SP4 ....
Love La *SAL* SP1 ....
Lovett Gn *SAL* SP1 ....
Lower Backway
   RSALW/SHRW SP3..................
Lower Folly *SALW/WIL* SP2 ....
Lower Rd *RSAL* SP5 ....
   RSAL SP5.............................
   SALW/WIL SP2 ....
Lower St *SALW/WIL* SP2 ....
Lumley Wk *AMSY* SP4 ....
Lynchets Rd *AMSY* SP4 ....
Lynchfield Rd *AMSY* SP4 ....
Lyndhurst Rd *AMSY* SP4 ....

M

Macklin Rd *SALW/WIL* SP2 ....
Maddington *RSALW/SHRW* SP3 ....
Main Rd *AMSY* SP4 ....
Mallard Cl *SALW/WIL* SP2 ....
Malthouse La *SALW/WIL* SP2 ....
The Maltings *SALW/WIL* SP2 ....
Malvern Wy *AMSY* SP4 ....
Manning Cl *SAL* SP1 ....
Manor Ct *SAL* * SP1 ....
Manor Farm La *SALW/WIL* SP2 ....
Manor Farm Rd *SAL* SP1..............
Manor Rd *SAL* SP1 ....
Maple Crs *SALW/WIL* SP2 ....
Maplecroft *SALW/WIL* SP2 ....
The Maples *SALW/WIL* * SP2........
Maple Wy *AMSY* SP4 ....
Marchment Cl *SALW/WIL* SP2 ......
Marie Av *AMSY* SP4.....................
Marina Cl *AMSY* SP4...................
Marina Crs *AMSY* SP4 ....
Marina Rd *AMSY* SP4 ....
   SAL SP1..............................
Markan Rd *AMSY* SP4 ....
Market Pl *SALW/WIL* SP2 ....
Market Wk *SALW/WIL* * SP2 ....
Marlborough Rd *AMSY* SP4 ....
   SAL SP1..............................
Marne Rd *AMSY* SP4 ....
Marsh La *RSAL* SP5....................
   SALW/WIL SP2 ....
Marshmead Cl *RSAL* SP5.............
Martins Cl *SALW/WIL* SP2 ....
Martlesham Rd *AMSY* SP4 ....
Maryland Cl *AMSY* SP4 ....
Matrons Cottages *RSAL* SP5 ....
Mayfair Rd *SAL* SP1 ....
McKie Rd *AMSY* SP4....................
McNeill Rd *AMSY* SP4 ....
Meadens La *RSAL* SP5 ....
Meadow Rd *AMSY* SP4 ....
   SALW/WIL SP2 ....
Meadow Rd South
   SALW/WIL SP2 ....
The Meadows *SAL* SP1 ....
Meads Rd *AMSY* SP4...................
Meadway *RSALW/SHRW* SP3 ....
Mears Rd *AMSY* SP4....................
Melbourne Gdns *AMSY* SP4 ....
Melvin Cl *SAL* SP1 ....
Merom Rw *SALW/WIL* * SP2 ....
Merrifield Rd *AMSY* SP4 ....
Mesh Pond *RSAL* SP5.................
Methuen Dr *SAL* SP1 ....
Meyrick Av *SALW/WIL* SP2 ....
Middle St *SALW/WIL* SP2 ....
Middleton Rd *SALW/WIL* SP2 ....

ord Hl *SAL* SP1 ......3 H5
ord Hollow *SAL* SP1 ......3 K5
ord Manor Gdns *SAL* SP1 ......30 A2
ord Mill Rd *SAL* SP1 ......30 A2
ord Pk *SAL* SP1 ......30 A3
ord St *SAL* SP1 ......3 G5
rook *SAL* SP1 ......3 J4
Cl *AMSY* SP4 ......16 A5
ennium Cl *SALW/WIL* SP2 ......29 C5
ennium Wy *SALW/WIL* SP2 ......29 C5
er Cl *SAL* SP1 ......23 H2
green Rd *AMSY* SP4 ......11 E4
La *SAL* SP1 ......32 D5
L SP1 ......23 H2
Race Cl *SALW/WIL* * SP2 ......2 C4
La *SAL* SP1 ......2 D5
Road Ms *SALW/WIL* * SP2 ......2 D4
Stream Ap *SALW/WIL* SP2 ......3 F3
s Wy *AMSY* SP4 ......11 F2
e Crs *AMSY* SP4 ......6 B3
e Rd *AMSY* SP4 ......9 E4
ton Rd *AMSY* SP4 ......8 B1
ton Vw *AMSY* SP4 ......8 A1
on Rd *AMSY* SP4 ......11 F4
LW/WIL SP2 ......29 C4
ster St *SAL* SP1 ......3 F5
LW/WIL SP2 ......22 B4
hell Rd *SALW/WIL* SP2 ......28 C2
hells Cl *RSAL* SP5 ......41 G3
erly Rd *SAL* SP1 ......24 B4
s Av *AMSY* SP4 ......9 E3
tague Rd *SALW/WIL* SP2 ......28 C3
nt Pleasant
tgomery Gdns
xton Cl *SAL* SP1 ......23 G5
xton Cl *SAL* SP1 ......25 E2
t Cl *RSAL* SP5 ......40 D3
t Gdns *RSAL* SP5 ......40 C3
t La *RSAL* SP5 ......40 C3
gan's La *AMSY* SP4 ......18 D2
gans Rise Rd *RSAL* SP5 ......41 G2
gans Vale Rd *RSAL* SP5 ......41 G3
Mount *SALW/WIL* * SP2 ......28 D5
nt La *RSALW/SHRW* SP3 ......20 A1
nt Pleasant
SALW/SHRW SP3 ......13 C2
yne Gdns *AMSY* SP4 ......11 F3
berry Wk *SAL* * SP1 ......3 J4
rfield *SAL* SP1 ......25 E2

N

der La *SALW/WIL* SP2 ......22 C5
der Ter *SALW/WIL* * SP2 ......2 B4
LW/WIL SP2 ......21 H5
ier Crs *SAL* SP1 ......30 A1
Cl *SAL* SP1 ......24 D2
son Cl *AMSY* SP4 ......9 H2
son Cl *AMSY* SP4 ......2 E2
heravon Rd *AMSY* SP4 ......7 G2
L SP1 ......3 H1
herhampton Rd
......27 C2
son Cl *SALW/WIL* SP2 ......32 C5
t Rd *RSALW/SHRW* SP3 ......4 B4
ille Cl *SAL* SP1 ......24 D3
v Bridge Rd *SAL* SP1 ......29 F3
v Bridge Rbt *SAL* SP1 ......29 G3
v Canal *SAL* SP1 ......3 F5
v Haig Rd *AMSY* SP4 ......9 G3
v Harnham Rd
LW/WIL SP2 ......29 F4
mans Wy *AMSY* SP4 ......8 C4
v Pines *RSAL* * SP5 ......39 E4
v Rd *AMSY* SP4 ......7 H2
v St *SAL* SP1 ......3 F5
vton Rd *SALW/WIL* SP2 ......28 C1
v Ward Rd *AMSY* SP4 ......9 E3
v Zealand Av *SALW/WIL* SP2 ......23 G5
olson Cl *AMSY* SP4 ......11 G3
htingale Wk *SALW/WIL* SP2 ......2 A1
folk Rd *SALW/WIL* SP2 ......28 C3
th Charford Crossing
BDG SP6 ......40 A5
then Ter *AMSY* SP4 ......6 D2
th Rd *AMSY* SP4 ......11 G4
thside *AMSY* SP4 ......18 A4
th St *SALW/WIL* SP2 ......2 D4
LW/WIL SP2 ......22 A4
v Wk *SAL* SP1 ......3 F6
thway *AMSY* SP4 ......17 G2
ton Dr *AMSY* SP4 ......18 A5
sery La *RSAL* SP5 ......10 D3
sery Rd *SALW/WIL* SP2 ......2 A3

O

Oak Ash Gn *SALW/WIL* SP2 ......21 H5
The Oakbournes *SAL* SP1 ......24 D2
Oak Cl *SALW/WIL* SP2 ......13 D4
Oak Dr *RSAL* SP5 ......38 C2
Oaklea La *RSAL* SP5 ......38 D3
Oak Pl *AMSY* SP4 ......11 E1
Oak Vw *SALW/WIL* * SP2 ......13 B3
Oakwood Gv *RSAL* SP5 ......38 C2
Odstock Rd *SALW/WIL* SP2 ......29 G5
Old Blandford Rd *RSAL* SP5 ......34 C4
SALW/WIL SP2 ......28 D5
Old Castle Rd *SAL* SP1 ......24 B1
Old Chapel Cl *RSAL* SP5 ......38 C2
Old Coach Rd *AMSY* SP4 ......8 D3
Oldfield *AMSY* SP4 ......24 D2
Old George Ml *SAL* * SP1 ......3 F5
Old Granary La *AMSY* SP4 ......10 C3
Old Malthouse La *AMSY* SP4 ......18 D5
Old Meadows Wk *SALW/WIL* SP2 ......2 A7
Old Rd *RSAL* SP5 ......38 B1
Old Shaftesbury Dro
SALW/WIL SP2 ......26 B4
Old Shaftsbury Dro
......28 C5
Old St *SALW/WIL* SP2 ......29 F4
Old Ward Rd *AMSY* SP4 ......8 D3
Olivier Cl *SALW/WIL* SP2 ......23 F2
Olivier Rd *SALW/WIL* SP2 ......21 G2
The Orchard *SAL* SP1 ......3 J1
Orchard End *AMSY* SP4 ......8 B3
Orchard Pl *SALW/WIL* * SP2 ......2 C3
Orchard Rd *RSAL* SP5 ......41 G2
SALW/WIL SP2 ......11 E3
Orchard Wy *AMSY* SP4 ......11 E3
Orford Rd *AMSY* SP4 ......11 F4
Owlswood *SAL* SP1 ......29 F5
Ox Rw *SAL* SP1 ......3 F5

P

The Packway *AMSY* SP4 ......6 C2
Paddock Cl *AMSY* SP4 ......19 E2
Paddock Wy *SAL* SP1 ......25 F5
Paddock Wood Cl *AMSY* SP4 ......7 H2
Pains Wy *AMSY* SP4 ......11 E4
Palmer Rd *AMSY* SP4 ......2 B1
The Paragon *SALW/WIL* * SP2 ......2 C3
Park Cl *SAL* SP1 ......24 B3
Parkland Wy *AMSY* SP4 ......16 C3
Park La *RSAL* SP5 ......37 E1
SAL SP1 ......24 B4
Park Rd *SAL* SP1 ......25 F5
Park St *SAL* SP1 ......3 H2
Parsonage Cl *SAL* SP1 ......23 H2
Parsonage Gn *SALW/WIL* SP2 ......23 H2
Parsonage Rd *AMSY* SP4 ......10 D3
Parsons Cl *AMSY* SP4 ......16 C4
Parsons Gn *RSALW/SHRW* SP3 ......4 A4
Paul's Dene Crs *SAL* SP1 ......24 C3
Paul's Dene Rd *SAL* SP1 ......24 B2
Payne's Hl *SAL* SP1 ......3 H6
Pearce Wy *SAL* SP1 ......25 E2
Pembroke Rd *SALW/WIL* SP2 ......23 F4
Penning Rd *SALW/WIL* SP2 ......23 E3
Pennings Dro *RSAL* SP5 ......34 D5
Pennyfarthing St *SAL* SP1 ......3 G4
Penny's La *SALW/WIL* SP2 ......22 A4
Penruddock Cl *SALW/WIL* SP2 ......23 F4
Pepperbox Ri *RSAL* SP5 ......39 E3
Petersfinger Rd *SAL* SP1 ......30 A2
Petticoat La *RSAL* SP5 ......41 H2
Philip Rd *AMSY* SP4 ......23 H1
SALW/WIL SP2 ......21 G2
Phillips La *AMSY* SP4 ......23 H1
Pilgrims Md *SAL* SP1 ......24 D2
Pilots Vw *AMSY* SP4 ......11 H5
Pinckneys Wy *AMSY* SP4 ......7 G2
Pineview Cl *RSAL* SP5 ......39 E5
Pinewoods Cl *SALW/WIL* SP2 ......23 E3
Pinewood Wy *SALW/WIL* SP2 ......23 E3
Pitts La *RSAL* SP5 ......32 D5
Pointers Wy *AMSY* SP4 ......11 F3
Polden Rd *SAL* SP1 ......3 K7
Poole Cl *SALW/WIL* * SP2 ......29 H5
Poores Rd *AMSY* SP4 ......7 H2
Poplar Wy *SAL* SP1 ......24 D2
Portfield Rd *SAL* SP1 ......26 B5
Portland Av *SALW/WIL* SP2 ......29 E5
Porton Rd *AMSY* SP4 ......11 F3
Portway *AMSY* SP4 ......18 B2
Potters Wy *SAL* SP1 ......30 A1
Power Rd *AMSY* SP4 ......6 B1

Pownall Rd *AMSY* SP4 ......7 E3
Primrose Hl *SALW/WIL* SP2 ......22 A3
Primrose La *RSAL* SP5 ......41 F3
Primrose Rd *SALW/WIL* SP2 ......23 F3
Princes Cl *RSAL* SP5 ......41 H2
Princes Hl *RSAL* SP5 ......41 H2
Priory Cl *RSAL* SP5 ......39 E3
RSALW/SHRW SP3 ......4 A4
SALW/WIL SP2 ......21 H5
Priory Sq *SALW/WIL* SP2 ......2 E4
Prospect Pl *SAL* * SP1 ......3 H6
SAL SP1 ......2 C2
Pullman Dr *AMSY* SP4 ......23 E4
Purvis Cl *AMSY* SP4 ......11 G3

Q

Quavey Rd *RSAL* SP5 ......41 H3
Queen Alexandra Rd
SALW/WIL SP2 ......23 F5
Queen Manor Rd *RSAL* SP5 ......30 B2
Queen Mary Rd *SALW/WIL* SP2 ......23 G4
Queensberry Rd *AMSY* SP4 ......11 E2
SAL SP1 ......24 B4
Queens Rd *SAL* SP1 ......3 G2
Queen St *SAL* SP1 ......3 G4
SALW/WIL SP2 ......22 A3

R

Radcliffe Rd *SALW/WIL* SP2 ......29 F4
Radnor Rd *SAL* SP1 ......24 B3
Raleigh Crs *AMSY* SP4 ......11 G3
Rambridge Crs *SALW/WIL* SP2 ......23 E2
Ramleaze Dr *SALW/WIL* SP2 ......23 F2
Rampart Rd *SAL* SP1 ......3 H4
Randall's Croft Rd
SALW/WIL SP2 ......21 G5
Ratfyn Rd *AMSY* SP4 ......10 D2
Ravenscroft *SALW/WIL* SP2 ......29 F5
Rawlence Rd *SALW/WIL* SP2 ......21 H5
SALW/WIL SP2 ......23 E4
Rawlinson Rd *AMSY* SP4 ......9 F3
Recreation Rd *SALW/WIL* SP2 ......7 H1
AMSY SP4 ......10 B3
Rectory La *RSAL* SP5 ......38 D3
Rectory Rd *RSAL* SP5 ......38 D3
SALW/WIL SP2 ......2 D5
Redford Cl *SAL* * SP1 ......25 E4
Reed Wk *AMSY* SP4 ......8 A2
Richards Wy *SALW/WIL* SP2 ......28 C3
Richmond Rd *SALW/WIL* SP2 ......2 C1
The Ridge *RSAL* SP5 ......41 G5
Ridgeway Rd *SAL* SP1 ......3 G1
Ridgmount *AMSY* SP4 ......7 H1
Ringwood Av *AMSY* SP4 ......11 E3
Riverbourne Rd *SAL* SP1 ......30 A1
Rivermead *AMSY* SP4 ......17 E1
Riverside *SAL* SP1 ......22 A4
Riverside Cl *SAL* SP1 ......25 E5
SALW/WIL SP2 ......13 C2
Riverside Rd *SAL* SP1 ......30 A1
Riverside Ter *RSALW/SHRW* SP3 ......12 B4
River Wy *SALW/WIL* SP2 ......8 A2
Robbins Rdg *AMSY* SP4 ......11 E4
Roberts Rd *SAL* SP1 ......23 G4
Robin Hill La *AMSY* SP4 ......8 A3
Rollestone Rd *RSALW/SHRW* SP3 ......4 A5
Rollestone St *SAL* SP1 ......3 G4
Roman Rd *AMSY* SP4 ......23 G5
Romer Rd *SALW/WIL* SP2 ......29 F4
Romsey Rd *AMSY* SP4 ......11 F4
Rosemary Cl *SALW/WIL* SP2 ......30 A1
Rosemary La *SAL* SP1 ......3 F6
Ross Rd *SALW/WIL* SP2 ......6 A1
Rougemont Cl *SAL* SP1 ......3 H4
The Row *RSAL* SP5 ......41 H2
RSALW/SHRW * SP3 ......12 C1
Rowan Cl *AMSY* SP4 ......7 G1
SALW/WIL SP2 ......23 E3
Rowbarrow Cl *SALW/WIL* SP2 ......29 G5
Rowbarrow *SALW/WIL* SP2 ......29 G5
Russell Rd *SALW/WIL* SP2 ......2 B2
Russell St *SALW/WIL* SP2 ......22 A4

S

Saddlers Md *SALW/WIL* SP2 ......21 H4
St Albans Cl *SAL* SP1 ......25 E2
St Andrews *SAL* SP1 ......25 E5
St Andrew's Cl *SALW/WIL* SP2 ......21 G5
St Andrew's Rd *SALW/WIL* SP2 ......13 D4

SALW/WIL SP2 ......23 F5
St Annes Cl *AMSY* SP4 ......11 E2
St Ann Pl *SAL* SP1 ......3 G6
St Ann St *SAL* SP1 ......3 G6
St Bedes Cl *SAL* SP1 ......25 E2
St Christophers Cl *SAL* SP1 ......25 E2
St Clair Rd *SALW/WIL* SP2 ......29 G4
St Clements Wy *SAL* SP1 ......24 D2
St Davids Cl *SAL* SP1 ......25 E2
St Edith's Cl *SALW/WIL* SP2 ......26 D1
St Edmund's Church St *SAL* SP1 ......3 G3
St Edwards Meadow *AMSY* SP4 ......19 E2
Saintes Cl *SAL* SP1 ......24 D2
St Francis Crs *SAL* SP1 ......24 C2
St Francis Rd *SAL* SP1 ......24 B3
St Georges Cl *SALW/WIL* * SP2 ......2 B7
St George's Rd *SALW/WIL* SP2 ......28 C3
St Gregory's Av *SALW/WIL* SP2 ......23 G5
St James Cl *SAL* SP1 ......25 E2
St John's Cl *SAL* SP1 ......30 A2
St John's Ct *SALW/WIL* SP2 ......21 H3
St John's St *SAL* SP1 ......3 G6
St Judes Cl *SAL* SP1 ......25 E3
St Lawrence Cl *SAL* SP1 ......23 H2
St Leonard's Cl *AMSY* SP4 ......8 B3
St Lukes Cl *SAL* SP1 ......25 E2
St Margaret's Cl *SAL* SP1 ......3 J5
St Mark's Av *SAL* SP1 ......24 C4
St Mark's Rd *SAL* SP1 ......3 H2
St Mark's Rbt *SAL* SP1 ......3 J2
St Martin's *SAL* SP1 ......3 H6
St Mary's Cl *SALW/WIL* SP2 ......26 C1
St Mary's Ct *SALW/WIL* * SP2 ......2 D3
St Mary's Rd *SALW/WIL* SP2 ......29 E3
St Matthews Cl *SAL* SP1 ......25 E2
St Michael's Cl *SALW/WIL* SP2 ......26 C1
St Michael's Rd *SALW/WIL* SP2 ......23 F3
St Nicholas Cl *SALW/WIL* SP2 ......26 C1
St Nicholas' Rd *SALW/WIL* SP2 ......3 G3
St Osmund's Cl *SAL* SP1 ......24 B2
St Pauls Homes *SALW/WIL* * SP2 ......2 D3
St Paul's Rd *SALW/WIL* SP2 ......2 D3
St Paul's Rbt *SALW/WIL* SP2 ......2 C3
St Peter's Cl *SALW/WIL* SP2 ......21 H5
St Peters Rd *SAL* SP1 ......24 D2
St Teresas Cl *SAL* SP1 ......24 D2
St Thomas's Sq *SALW/WIL* * SP2 ......3 F4
St Thomas Wy *SAL* SP1 ......25 E2
St Ursula's Cl *SAL* SP1 ......25 E3
Salisbury Rd *AMSY* SP4 ......8 B5
AMSY SP4 ......10 D3
RSAL SP5 ......34 C3
RSALW/SHRW SP3 ......4 A4
SALW/WIL SP2 ......22 B4
Salisbury St *AMSY* SP4 ......10 C3
Salt La *AMSY* SP4 ......19 F1
SAL SP1 ......3 G4
Sandown Pl *SALW/WIL* SP2 ......2 D4
The Sandringhams *RSAL* SP5 ......39 E4
Sandy La *RSAL* SP5 ......41 H2
Sarum Cl *SALW/WIL* SP2 ......23 H4
Saxonhurst *RSAL* SP5 ......40 D3
Saxon Rd *SALW/WIL* SP2 ......29 E4
School Dr *AMSY* SP4 ......7 H2
School Hl *RSAL* SP5 ......38 B3
School La *AMSY* SP4 ......10 D2
SAL SP1 ......3 G3
School Rd *AMSY* SP4 ......8 A1
Scots La *SAL* SP1 ......3 G3
Seagrim Rd *SALW/WIL* SP2 ......21 H5
Senior Dr *SALW/WIL* SP2 ......29 F5
Seth Ward Dr *SAL* SP1 ......25 E4
Shady Bower *SAL* SP1 ......3 K5
Shady Bower Cl *SAL* SP1 ......3 K5
Shaftesbury Rd
RSALW/SHRW SP3 ......20 A4
SALW/WIL SP2 ......21 G4
Shakespeare Pl *SALW/WIL* * SP2 ......2 D3
Shakespeare Rd *SAL* SP1 ......24 A3
Sharrat Av *SAL* SP1 ......24 D2
Sheen Rd *SALW/WIL* SP2 ......23 E2
Sheepbridge Rd *AMSY* SP4 ......9 F1
Shelley Dr *SAL* SP1 ......24 A3
Shepherds Cl *RSAL* SP5 ......34 D4
RSAL SP5 ......36 B5
Sherfield *SAL* SP1 ......18 D2
Shortlands *SALW/WIL* SP2 ......21 G4
Short La *RSALW/SHRW* SP3 ......20 A3
Shrapnel Rd *AMSY* SP4 ......6 A2
Shropshire Cl *SALW/WIL* SP2 ......23 F2
Shute End Rd *RSAL* SP5 ......37 H1
RSAL SP5 ......38 B4
Shutts La *RSAL* SP5 ......34 D4
The Sidings *RSAL* SP5 ......40 D1
Sidney St *SALW/WIL* SP2 ......2 D3
Signal St *AMSY* SP4 ......9 F4
Silver St *RSAL* SP5 ......38 A2
SAL SP1 ......3 F5

SALW/WIL SP2 ....22 A4
Silver Wd *RSAL* SP5 ....38 B2
Silverwood Dr *SAL* SP1 ....25 F5
Simmance Wy *AMSY* SP4 ....11 E3
Skew Bridge Rd *SALW/WIL* SP2 ....23 G5
Skew Rd *SALW/WIL* SP2 ....22 D5
Slab La *RSAL* SP5 ....40 D2
Sling Rd *AMSY* SP4 ....9 F2
Smeaton Rd *SALW/WIL* SP2 ....2 B4
Smithfield St *AMSY* SP4 ....10 D3
Solstice Ri *AMSY* SP4 ....10 D3
Somerset Rd *SAL* SP1 ....24 C4
Southampton Rd *RSAL* SP5 ....38 B2
SAL SP1 ....3 J7
Southbourne Cl *AMSY* SP4 ....16 C3
Southbourne Wy *AMSY* SP4 ....16 C3
South La *RSAL* SP5 ....40 B2
Southmill Hl *AMSY* SP4 ....10 D5
South Mill Rd *AMSY* SP4 ....10 D4
South St *SALW/WIL* SP2 ....2 D5
SALW/WIL SP2 ....13 C3
SALW/WIL SP2 ....26 D1
South Vw *RSALW/SHRW* * SP3 ....4 B4
Southway *AMSY* SP4 ....17 C2
South Wy *AMSY* SP5 ....38 D3
South Western Rd
SALW/WIL SP2 ....2 C4
Spiders Island *RSAL* SP5 ....39 E3
Springfield Crs *RSAL* SP5 ....41 G4
Squarey Cl *AMSY* SP4 ....40 C3
Stanley Little Rd *SALW/WIL* SP2 ...23 E4
Station Rd *SALW/WIL* SP2 ....13 B3
Station Ter *SALW/WIL* SP2 ....2 C3
The Steadings *AMSY* SP4 ....25 E1
Stephens Cl *SALW/WIL* SP2 ....28 D3
Stephenson Rd *SALW/WIL* SP2 ....2 B5
Stockport Rd *AMSY* SP4 ....11 F5
Stocks Bridge La *RSAL* SP5 ....34 D4
Stockwood Cl *SAL* SP1 ....24 D4
Stoford Br *SALW/WIL* SP2 ....13 C3
Stoneavon *SAL* * SP4 ....7 G2
Stonehenge Rd *AMSY* SP4 ....7 G2
AMSY SP4 ....10 A2
Stratford Br *SALW/WIL* SP2 ....23 G1
Stratford Rd *SAL* SP1 ....23 H2
Stratford Tony Rd *RSAL* SP5 ....34 B3
St Thomas's Br *SAL* SP1 ....25 G2
The Styles *RSAL* SP5 ....32 D5
Suffolk Rd *SALW/WIL* SP2 ....28 D4
Summerlock Ap *SALW/WIL* SP2 ....2 E4
Sunnyhill Rd *SAL* SP1 ....24 B3
Sussex Rd *SALW/WIL* SP2 ....28 C4
Suvla La *AMSY* SP4 ....9 E3
Swallowmead *SALW/WIL* SP2 ....29 F5
Swan Cl *AMSY* SP4 ....8 A2
SALW/WIL SP2 ....29 F4
Swattons Cl *AMSY* SP4 ....8 C3
Swayne Rd *SALW/WIL* SP2 ....26 D1

Swaynes Cl *SAL* SP1 ....3 G2
Swiftdown *SALW/WIL* SP2 ....29 F5
Sycamore Dr *SAL* SP1 ....24 D2
Syringa Ct *SALW/WIL* * SP2 ....28 C1

T

Talbot Cl *SAL* SP1 ....24 D3
Tanners Cl *AMSY* SP4 ....18 D3
Tanners Fld *AMSY* SP4 ....11 F3
Tanners La *AMSY* SP4 ....18 D3
RSALW/SHRW SP3 ....4 A4
Tempest Rd *AMSY* * SP4 ....11 F3
Thistlebarrow Rd *SAL* SP1 ....24 B3
Thompson Cl *SALW/WIL* SP2 ....29 E5
Thorne Cl *RSAL* SP5 ....34 C4
Thorneydown Rd *AMSY* SP4 ....19 F1
Thornton Crs *SALW/WIL* SP2 ....22 C3
Three Cuppes La *SAL* SP1 ....3 G4
Thurlow St *SALW/WIL* SP2 ....11 G3
Tidworth Rd *AMSY* SP4 ....9 F2
AMSY SP4 ....16 C3
Tinneys Cl *RSAL* SP5 ....41 G5
Tollgate Cl *AMSY* SP4 ....10 C1
Tollgate Rd *SAL* SP1 ....3 H6
Tombs Rd *AMSY* SP4 ....7 E3
Tournament Rd *SALW/WIL* SP2 .....23 F4
Towell Rd *AMSY* SP4 ....7 E3
Tower Ms *SAL* SP1 ....3 H1
Town Pth *SALW/WIL* SP2 ....2 B7
Trenchard Av *AMSY* SP4 ....19 F2
Trinity Rd *RSALW/SHRW* SP3 ....4 B3
Trinity St *SAL* SP1 ....3 G6
Tryhorn Dr *SAL* SP1 ....24 C2
Tucker Cl *AMSY* SP4 ....11 E4
Tunnel Hl *RSAL* SP5 ....38 B3
Turner Cl *SALW/WIL* SP2 ....2 A7
Twineham Gdns *RSAL* SP5 ....38 D3
Twynham Cl *RSAL* SP5 ....40 C3
Tylers Cl *SALW/WIL* SP2 ....28 C3
Tyrone Av *AMSY* SP4 ....9 E2

U

Underwood Dr *AMSY* SP4 ....11 F4
Upper Backway
RSALW/SHRW SP3 ....4 B3
Upper Folly *SALW/WIL* SP2 ....26 C1
Upper St *SALW/WIL* SP2 ....28 C3

V

Vale Rd *RSAL* SP5 ....41 G3

Vale View Rd *SALW/WIL* SP2 ....13 D4
The Valley *SALW/WIL* SP2 ....23 F3
Valley Cl *RSAL* SP5 ....41 G3
Vanessa Av *SAL* SP1 ....30 A1
The Ventry *SAL* SP1 ....3 H1
Vernon Cl *AMSY* SP4 ....11 G3
Verona Rd *SAL* SP1 ....24 A3
Vicarage Pk *RSAL* SP5 ....41 G3
Victoria Cl *SALW/WIL* SP2 ....21 H4
Victoria Ct *SAL* SP1 ....24 B4
Victoria Rd *SAL* SP1 ....24 B4
SALW/WIL SP2 ....21 H4
Viking Wy *SALW/WIL* SP2 ....29 G5
Vimy Crs *AMSY* SP4 ....9 E5
Virginia Cl *AMSY* SP4 ....11 F3

W

Wain-a-Long Rd *SAL* SP1 ....3 J2
Waleran Cl *RSAL* SP5 ....38 D3
Warminster Rd *SALW/WIL* SP2 ......22 A2
Warwick Cl *SAL* SP1 ....24 A4
Washern Cl *SALW/WIL* SP2 ....26 D1
Wason Rd *AMSY* SP4 ....6 B3
Water Ditchampton
SALW/WIL SP2 ....21 H2
Watergate La *AMSY* SP4 ....7 H4
Water La *SALW/WIL* SP2 ....2 D4
Waterloo Rd *SAL* SP1 ....3 J7
Watersmeet Rd *SALW/WIL* SP2 ....29 F4
Waters Rd *SAL* SP1 ....24 B3
Water St *AMSY* SP4 ....8 B3
Watson Rd *AMSY* SP4 ....6 B2
Watt Rd *SALW/WIL* SP2 ....28 C2
Wavell Rd *SALW/WIL* SP2 ....29 F4
Waverley Pl *SAL* * SP1 ....3 G5
Weeke Cl *RSAL* SP5 ....40 A2
Wellington Rd *AMSY* SP4 ....9 G2
Wellington Wy *SALW/WIL* SP2 ......23 G4
Wells Cl *AMSY* SP4 ....7 F3
Wells Rd *AMSY* SP4 ....7 F4
Wessex Rd *SAL* SP1 ....3 J4
SALW/WIL SP2 ....26 C1
Westbourne Cl *SAL* SP1 ....3 K5
West End Rd *AMSY* SP4 ....2 A2
Western Wy *SALW/WIL* SP2 ....23 E4
Westfield Cl *AMSY* SP4 ....2 A3
SAL SP1 ....25 E5
Westland Cl *AMSY* SP4 ....11 F3
Westminster Rd *SALW/WIL* SP2 .....2 C1
West St *SALW/WIL* SP2 ....2 D4
SALW/WIL SP2 ....13 B2
SALW/WIL SP2 ....21 H4
West Street Pl *SALW/WIL* * SP2 ......2 D4
West Wk *SAL* SP1 ....2 E2
Westwood Rd *SALW/WIL* SP2 ....23 E3
Whinyates Rd *AMSY* SP4 ....6 B2

Whitbred Rd *SALW/WIL* SP2 2
Whitchers Meadow *RSAL* SP5 3
Whitebridge Rd *SALW/WIL* SP1 ......
Whitefriars Rd *SAL* SP1 ....
Whitesbury Rd *RSAL* SP5 3
Whiteshoot Hl *RSAL* SP5 4
Whitlock Ri *RSAL* SP5 ....
Whittle Rd *SALW/WIL* SP2 2
Wilcot Cl *AMSY* SP4 ....
Wiley Ter *SALW/WIL* SP2 ....
William Cl *SAL* SP1 ....
Willoughby Rd *AMSY* SP4 ....
Willow Cl *SAL* SP1 ....
Willow Dr *AMSY* SP4 ....
The Willows *SALW/WIL* * SP2 2
Wilman Wy *SALW/WIL* SP2 2
Wilson Rd *AMSY* SP4 ....
Wilton Rd *RSALW/SHRW* SP3 ....
SALW/WIL SP2 ....
Wiltshire Cl *AMSY* SP4 ....
Wiltshire Rd *SALW/WIL* SP2 ....
Winchester Cl *AMSY* SP4 1
Winchester St *SAL* SP1 ....
Winding Wy *SALW/WIL* SP2 2
Windlesham Rd *SAL* SP1 ....
Windmill Cl *RSAL* SP5 ....
Windmill La *AMSY* SP4 1
Windsor Ms *AMSY* SP4 ....
Windsor Rd *AMSY* SP4 ....
SALW/WIL SP2 ....
Windsor St *SALW/WIL* SP2 ....
Windwhistle Wy *RSAL* SP5 ....
Wing Rd *AMSY* SP4 ....
Winterslow Rd *AMSY* SP4 1
Wishford Rd *SALW/WIL* SP2 2
Witherington Rd *RSAL* SP5 3
Wittenham Vw *AMSY* SP4 1
Wolferstan Dr *SAL* SP1 ....
Woodbury Gdns *SALW/WIL* SP2 .....
Woodland Wy *SAL* SP1 ....
Woodlea Gra *RSAL* SP5 ....
Wood Rd *AMSY* SP4 ....
Woodside Rd *SALW/WIL* SP2 ....
Woodstock Rd *SAL* SP1 ....
Woodvill Rd *SAL* SP1 ....
Wordsworth Rd *SAL* SP1 ....
Wrenscroft *SALW/WIL* SP2 ....
Wylye Ldg *SALW/WIL* * SP2 2
Wyndham Pk *SAL* SP1 ....
Wyndham Rd *SAL* SP1 ....
Wyndham Ter *SAL* SP1 ....
Wyvern Rd *AMSY* SP4 ....

Y

Yewtree Cl *AMSY* SP4 ....
York Rd *SALW/WIL* SP2 ....

Index - featured places

Alderbury Caravan &
  Camping Park
  RSAL SP5 ....39 E5
Alderbury & West
  Grimstead School
  RSAL SP5 ....38 D2
Allenbrooke Barracks
  AMSY SP4 ....6 C1
All Saints CE Infant School
  AMSY SP4 ....8 A1
Amesbury Abbey
  AMSY SP4 ....10 C2
Amesbury CE Junior School
  AMSY SP4 ....10 D2
Amesbury Health Centre
  AMSY SP4 ....10 D3
Amesbury Industrial Estate
  AMSY SP4 ....11 E1
Amesbury Infant School
  AMSY SP4 ....10 D2
Amesbury Sports Centre
  AMSY SP4 ....11 E2
Appleford School
  RSALW/SHRW * SP3 ....4 A2
Ashfield Road Trading Estate
  SALW/WIL SP2 ....2 A3
The Avenue
  AMSY SP4 ....6 C5
Avondale School
  AMSY SP4 ....8 B3
Avon Middle School
  SALW/WIL SP2 ....23 G3

Barnack Business Centre
  SAL SP1 ....3 J6
Barnack Business Park
  SAL SP1 ....3 J6
Barnack Industrial Estate
  SALW/WIL SP2 ....22 A3
Belmont School
  SAL SP1 ....3 G3
Bemerton Heath
  Harlequins FC
  SALW/WIL SP2 ....23 E4
Bemerton St Johns CE
  First School
  SALW/WIL SP2 ....28 B1
Bishop Wordsworths School
  SAL SP1 ....3 F6
Boathouse Meadow
  Business Park
  SALW/WIL SP2 ....28 C1
Boscombe Down
  Business Park
  AMSY SP4 ....11 E2
Bourne Retail Park
  SAL SP1 ....30 A3
Britford CE Primary School
  RSAL SP5 ....30 A5
Bulford CE Primary School
  AMSY SP4 ....8 C3
Bulford Kiwi Primary School
  AMSY SP4 ....9 F3
Central Health Clinic
  SALW/WIL SP2 ....2 E3

Chafyn Grove School
  SAL SP1 ....3 J2
Christ the King RC
  Primary School
  AMSY SP4 ....10 D3
Churchfields Industrial Estate
  SALW/WIL SP2 ....2 A4
Clarendon Palace
  RSAL SP5 ....31 F1
Coombe Bissett CE
  First School
  RSAL SP5 ....34 C4
Coombe Touring Park
  SALW/WIL SP2 ....27 E4
Cross Keys Shopping Centre
  SAL SP1 ....3 G4
The Cursus
  AMSY SP4 ....6 A5
David Hart Business Centre
  RSAL SP5 ....40 B1
Dolphin Industrial Estate
  SAL SP1 ....3 K7
Down House
  RSAL SP5 ....41 G1
Downton CE Primary School
  RSAL SP5 ....40 B1
Downton Industrial Estate
  RSAL SP5 ....40 B1
Downton Secondary School
  RSAL SP5 ....40 B2
Durrington CE Junior School
  AMSY SP4 ....7 H2

Durrington Swimming Pool
  AMSY SP4 ....
Durrington Walls
  AMSY SP4 ....
Exeter House Special School
  SAL SP1 2
Farm Lane Business Centre
  SALW/WIL SP2 ....
Figsbury Ring
  AMSY SP4 1
Fisherton Manor
  Middle School
  SALW/WIL SP2 ....
Five Rivers Leisure Centre
  SAL SP1 2
The Godolphin School
  SAL SP1 ....
Gomeldon Primary School
  AMSY SP4 1
Gordon Barracks
  AMSY SP4 ....
Great Wishford CE
  First School
  SALW/WIL SP2 1
Greentrees Primary School
  SAL SP1 1
The Harcourt Medical Centre
  SALW/WIL SP2 ....
Harnham Gate
  SAL SP1 ....
Harnham J & I School
  SALW/WIL SP2 ....

...nham Trading Estate
...ALW/WIL SP2 .... 28 B3
...le Gardens
...lant Centre & Shop
...MSY SP4 .... 14 C5
...nbury First School
...ALW/WIL SP2 .... 2 B2
...h Post Golf Club
...MSY SP4 .... 15 H5
...h Street Gate
...AL SP1 .... 3 F6
...ne Barracks
...MSY SP4 .... 6 A1
...iston Primary School
...MSY SP4 .... 16 D3
...us House
...Salisbury &
...outh Wiltshire Museum)
... SP2 .... 2 D7
...gsway Business Centre
... SP2 .... 22 A3
...gsway Trading Estate
...ALW/WIL SP2 .... 22 B2
...l Barracks
...MSY SP4 .... 9 F3
...etraite Swan
...AL SP1 .... 3 H1
...hill Primary School
...MSY SP4 .... 6 B2
...den Hall School
...ALW/WIL SP2 .... 2 E7
...e Woodbury
...SAL SP5 .... 36 C1
...gford Castle
...SAL SP5 .... 37 H3
...mesbury House
...AL SP1 .... 3 F6
...kings Shopping Centre
...ALW/WIL SP2 .... 2 E4
...l Medieval Hall
...Secrets of Salisbury)
...ALW/WIL SP2 .... 2 D6
...Wessex Clinic
...ALW/WIL SP2 .... 2 A3
...ord Industrial Estate
...AL SP1 .... 3 K6
...ord Trading Estate
...AL SP1 .... 3 K6

Mompesson House
SALW/WIL SP2 .... 2 E5
Morgans Vale & Woodfalls CE
Primary School
RSAL SP5 .... 41 G2
Neale's Barrow
SALW/WIL SP2 .... 26 C4
Netherhampton
Business Centre
SALW/WIL SP2 .... 27 H2
New Hall Hospital
RSAL SP5 .... 37 G4
Odeon Cinema
... SP2 .... 3 F5
Odstock Primary School
RSAL SP5 .... 36 C4
Ogbury
AMSY SP4 .... 15 F1
Old George Mall
Shopping Centre
... SP1 .... 3 F5
The Old Manor Hospital
SALW/WIL SP2 .... 2 B3
Old Sarum
SAL SP1 .... 24 A1
Paxton Business Centre
SALW/WIL SP2 .... 28 C1
Pembroke Park First School
SALW/WIL SP2 .... 23 F4
Picton Barracks
AMSY SP4 .... 9 F4
Playhouse Theatre
SALW/WIL SP2 .... 2 E4
Roberts Barracks
AMSY SP4 .... 6 B2
Royal Aircraft Establishment
AMSY SP4 .... 6 B1
St Andrews CE Primary School
SAL SP1 .... 25 F4
St Ann's Gate
SAL SP1 .... 3 G6
St Edmunds CE Girls
School & Sports College
SAL SP1 .... 25 F4
St Josephs Catholic School
SAL SP1 .... 25 F4
St Mark's CE Junior School
SAL SP1 .... 24 C4

St Martins CE Infant School
SAL SP1 .... 3 H6
St Martins CE Junior School
SAL SP1 .... 3 J6
St Nicholas Hospital
SAL SP1 .... 29 F3
St Osmunds RC Primary School
SAL SP1 .... 3 G7
Salisbury Arts Centre
SAL SP1 .... 3 G3
Salisbury Athletics Track
SAL SP1 .... 24 A4
Salisbury Cathedral
SAL SP1 .... 3 F6
Salisbury Cathedral School
SAL SP1 .... 3 F7
Salisbury City Library &
Art Gallery
SAL SP1 .... 3 F4
Salisbury College
SAL SP1 .... 3 H6
Salisbury Crematorium
SAL SP1 .... 24 D4
Salisbury District Hospital
RSAL SP5 .... 36 D2
Salisbury Livestock Market
SALW/WIL SP2 .... 28 A3
Salisbury Racecourse
SALW/WIL SP2 .... 27 E5
Salisbury RFC
SAL SP1 .... 24 B3
Salisbury & South Wilts Golf Club
SALW/WIL SP2 .... 27 H3
Salisbury & South Wiltshire
Sports Club
SALW/WIL SP2 .... 23 F5
Sarum St Pauls CE (AV)
Primary School
SALW/WIL SP2 .... 2 B1
School of Artillery
AMSY SP4 .... 6 D1
Shrewton CE Primary School
RSALW/SHRW SP3 .... 4 A3
South Newton Industrial Estate
SALW/WIL SP2 .... 13 G4
South Wilts Girls
Grammar School
SAL SP1 .... 24 A4

Stapleford Castle (Ring & Bailey)
RSALW/SHRW SP3 .... 12 B4
Stirling Barracks
AMSY SP4 .... 7 E1
Stonehenge
AMSY SP4 .... 5 E1
The Stonehenge School
AMSY SP4 .... 10 D2
Stratford-sub-Castle
Primary School
SAL SP1 .... 23 G2
Upper Avon School
AMSY SP4 .... 8 A1
Ward Barracks
AMSY SP4 .... 9 E3
The Wardrobe
(Regimental Museum)
SALW/WIL SP2 .... 2 D6
Westwood St Thomas School
SALW/WIL SP2 .... 22 D3
Whaddon Business Park
RSAL SP5 .... 39 E4
Wilton CE First School
SALW/WIL SP2 .... 21 G5
Wilton CE Middle School
SALW/WIL SP2 .... 21 G3
Wilton Health Centre
SALW/WIL SP2 .... 22 A4
Wilton House
SALW/WIL SP2 .... 22 A5
The Wilton Shopping Village
SALW/WIL SP2 .... 22 A4
Wing Barracks
AMSY SP4 .... 9 E4
Winterbourne Earls CE
Primary School
AMSY SP4 .... 18 D3
Woodford Valley CE
Primary School
AMSY SP4 .... 14 A5
Woodhenge
AMSY SP4 .... 7 F4
Woodlands First School
SALW/WIL SP2 .... 23 E3
Wyndham Park Infant School
SAL SP1 .... 24 C4
Wyvern College
SAL SP1 .... 25 F4

Notes

AA Street by Street — QUESTIONNAIRE

Dear Atlas User
Your comments, opinions and recommendations are very important to us.
So please help us to improve our street atlases by taking a few minutes
to complete this simple questionnaire.

You do NOT need a stamp (unless posted outside the UK). If you do not want to remove this page from your street atlas, then photocopy it or write your answers on a plain sheet of paper.

Send to: The Editor, AA Street by Street, FREEPOST SCE 4598,
Basingstoke RG21 4GY

ABOUT THE ATLAS...

Which city/town/county did you buy?

_____

Are there any features of the atlas or mapping that you find particularly useful?

_____
_____
_____

Is there anything we could have done better?

_____
_____
_____

Why did you choose an AA Street by Street atlas?

_____
_____
_____

Did it meet your expectations?

Exceeded ☐   **Met all** ☐   **Met most** ☐   **Fell below** ☐

Please give your reasons

_____
_____
_____
_____
_____

ML

continued overleaf

Where did you buy it?

For what purpose? (please tick all applicable)

To use in your own local area ☐   To use on business or at work ☐

Visiting a strange place ☐   In the car ☐   On foot ☐

Other (please state)

LOCAL KNOWLEDGE...

Local knowledge is invaluable. Whilst every attempt has been made to make the information contained in this atlas as accurate as possible, should you notice any inaccuracies, please detail them below (if necessary, use a blank piece of paper) or e-mail us at *streetbystreet@theAA.com*

ABOUT YOU...

Name (Mr/Mrs/Ms)
Address

Postcode

Daytime tel no
E-mail address

Which age group are you in?

Under 25 ☐   25-34 ☐   35-44 ☐   45-54 ☐   55-64 ☐   65+ ☐

Are you an AA member?   YES ☐   NO ☐

Do you have Internet access?   YES ☐   NO ☐

Thank you for taking the time to complete this questionnaire. Please send it to us as soon as possible, and remember, you do not need a stamp (unless posted outside the UK).

ML